W9-CPJ-357

Tales from the
Detroit Tigers Dugout

JACK EBLING

SportsPublishingLLC.com

ISBN-10: 1-59670-193-5
ISBN-13: 978-1-59670-193-9

Publishers: Peter L. Bannon and Joseph J. Bannon Sr.
Senior managing editor: Susan M. Moyer
Acquisitions editor: Mike Pearson
Editor: Laura Podeschi
Art director: K. Jeffrey Higgerson
Cover design: Joseph Brumleve
Project manager: Kathryn R. Holleman
Photo editor: Erin Linden-Levy

Sports Publishing L.L.C.
804 North Neil Street
Champaign, IL 61820
Phone: 1-877-424-2665
Fax: 217-363-2073
www.SportsPublishingLLC.com

Printed in the United States of America

CIP data available upon request.

Contents

Acknowledgments
THE ASSISTS AND SACRIFICES

NO ONE PERSON can tell the story of a proud franchise. Fortunately, no individual needs to do that.

The 106-year history of the Detroit Tigers has been written by 1,431 players, 36 managers, and millions of dedicated fans.

Without them, this book doesn't happen. And it's time to salute them—the great and the sometimes good from more than a century of American League baseball.

Particular thanks to the 2006 Tigers, who made the game fun again. That credit starts at the top with Dave Dombrowski and Jim Leyland and filters down to the 25th man on the roster. Their passion for winning and Leyland's candor were much appreciated.

But there were others who helped immeasurably with their time and input:

- Brian Britten, Rick Thompson, and Elizabeth Allison of the Tigers media relations staff.

- Al Kaline and Willie Horton from the playing field and the front office.

- Ernie Harwell, Dan Dickerson, Mario Impemba, and Rod Allen from the broadcast booth.

- Jerry Green, Lynn Henning, Gary Gillette, Larry Lage, Mark Wilson, Shireen Saski, and dozens of other writers and broadcasters living and deceased.

Special thanks to Sports Publishing's Mike Pearson, who fought for this project, and Laura Podeschi, an editor with patience.

A tip of the cap to WILS' Chris Holman, a giver at all times, and Mac MacDonald, who never stopped asking, "Aren't you done with that book yet?"

Thanks to Jamie Bolt and Doug Warren for helping so much with my day job.

A special salute to "The 11"—and you know who you are. Without all of you, this wouldn't have been possible.

Mom, Dad, Nanc, Jim, Lynn, Earle, Andy, Grinz, Drew, Tom, and Dave—you'll never know how much you helped.

Finally, an apology to the rest of the Ebling family—Robin, Zach, Alison, and Mags. If I've been gone too much or buried at the computer, I hope you understand why.

–JACK EBLING

January 21, 2007

CHAPTER ONE

The Plan and The Man

HOW THE 2006 DETROIT TIGERS WERE BUILT

IT WAS A SIX-MONTH ROOT CANAL. Nearly every day meant a new drilling—119 in all. But that was four years ago. And after the careful brushing and flossing of a franchise, could any American League baseball team have a brighter smile than the Detroit Tigers?

Not if you ask their devoted fans. After setting club records with 26 sellouts and a regular-season attendance of 2,595,937, not counting six packed houses in postseason play, Detroit's turnaround in 2006 carried over to the turnstiles.

None of that could have happened without a major financial commitment from owner/director Mike Ilitch and tireless work from an unsung staff.

But unless we're talking about Ilitch's dreams, each big hit and clutch catch was made by a player. And the men who made those performances possible were president, CEO, and general manager Dave Dombrowski and his first choice to manage the Tigers, a motivated Jim Leyland.

"Jim and I go back a long time," Dombrowski said of a tandem that won the 1997 World Series with Florida. "If he has that fire and passion in his belly, Jim is one of the best in baseball. I had to see if he had that again. But he's not going to mislead you. He's going to tell you. And when he does, you're getting the consummate manager. He can be as tough as anyone when he has to be."

Tough jobs are everywhere. And when Dombrowski came to Detroit from the Marlins after the 2001 season, he took over a team that was 66-96. As president and CEO, he also inherited general manager Randy Smith and manager Phil Garner. Neither man made it to 2003 with the Tigers, as Dombrowski took on the GM duties and hired Luis Pujols, then fan favorite Alan Trammell, as manager.

"You have to go back to 2001," Dombrowski said. "We had to make intelligent observations and get people on board we could trust. The blueprint was similar to the one for Florida. But how we would get there was somewhat different. Here we needed to regroup and rebuild and develop a winning attitude. That can take a long time."

It took too long for everyone at Comerica Park except some grateful visiting teams. Detroit slipped to 55 wins in 2002, then to 43 the next year, nearly setting a major-league record for ineptitude. After a nice jump to 72 wins in 2004, a trip on the treadmill produced 71 victories and meant Trammell had done all he could.

"I feel bad for any manager who's fired," Leyland said. "And I feel particularly bad for Alan Trammell. He didn't really have a chance his last year. I've said it all along, if (Carlos) Guillen and 'Pudge' (Ivan Rodriguez) and (Magglio) Ordonez are out of our lineup on a consistent basis, we wouldn't be worth a shit either. That's the way it is. But people don't want to hear that."

Fans want to hear—or better yet, see—six things:

1. Their team's front office is aggressive and intelligent in making trades—without sacrificing their favorite players.

2. Their team is able to acquire important free agents without breaking the bank and having to raise ticket prices.

3. Their scouts and general manager can identify and sign top prospects to provide the hope of brighter days ahead.

4. Their team's manager can communicate with stars and scrubs, never coddling players or locking them in the doghouse.

5. Their manager's baseball decisions are sound, from his handling of pitchers to his preference for long ball or small ball.

6. Their team's oldest players still perform with off-the-wall passion, while the youngsters play a lot smarter than their years.

Oh, and one more thing. Their team needs to win much more than it loses and should play long after the first Sunday in October.

If that reads like a description of the '06 Tigers, it is. It also shows what can happen when an owner cares. In Ilitch's case, that meant building a new stadium, a heart-wrenching move, and hiring good people, then letting them work. He couldn't have won making baseball decisions with one hand in Little Caesar's pizza dough and the other squeezing a Detroit Red Wings hockey stick.

"It's great because this was Mr. Ilitch's grand plan when he envisioned leaving Tiger Stadium and staying in Detroit, instead of moving to the suburbs," said closer Todd Jones, who threw the last pitch at the corner of Michigan and Trumbull. "He wanted to put a good product on the field. And it's nice to see everything come together for him and see all the fans show up and support us."

Once the team had moved to Foxtown, the key decision was hiring Dombrowski, whose amazing memory has helped him win in a wide variety of situations.

"I remember Dave when he was a rookie in the front office with the White Sox," Hall of Fame broadcaster Ernie Harwell said. "He'd gone to Western Michigan. And he broke in under Roland Hemond and Paul Richards. He wasn't much more than a gofer at first, but he moved up quickly. They saw him the same way I did—as a hard-working guy who was very dedicated and had a lot of intelligence. He was trained in the old school, where they depended on scouting. But Dave always seemed to know who'd make it five or six years down the road."

His fifth year with the Tigers was his first year reunited with Leyland, whose self-deprecation and frank approach to problems was a perfect fit.

"There are a lot of teams I couldn't manage," Leyland said. "And I wouldn't be the right guy for a lot of teams. I hope I'm the right guy for this one. I don't know if I am or not. But I feel comfortable with Dave. I knew Dave. I knew the city. I knew it was a baseball town. I thought there was some talent here. I felt this was a good situation. Other places, I wouldn't have been asked to go. And I wouldn't have gone if I had been asked."

When asked about Trammell, the top shortstop in Detroit history, Leyland can never say enough nice things. And even if his team is 40 games over .500, as it was early last August, he won't suffer a dislocated shoulder from patting himself on the back.

"I know how tough this job is," Leyland said. "It's really tough if you don't have the players. When people see the dollar signs, they forget about that. But this is a hard job. There are only 30 of them. And there's a lot of pressure. That's just the way it is."

The job is tough enough and important enough that Dombrowski doesn't buy the idea, espoused by Hall of Famer Sparky Anderson and others, that the best manager might make a five-game difference in the standings.

"I don't believe that at all," Dombrowski said. "Sparky is just being humble when he says that. You have to be aware of how someone says it. With direct moves, that may be the case. But a manager can make the difference between a winning culture and a losing culture. He can make the difference between finishing last or first."

Guess what? So can a top-notch general manager, as Dombrowski proved to be with Montreal from 1988-1991 and Florida for the decade that followed. Beginning at age 31, he showed he could build a team via the farm system or with high-priced free agents.

"One thing you have to do is look at players on an individual basis and see who is going to continue to grow," he said. "Is there someone three or four years down the road who can upgrade your talent? And I'd say there's always an emphasis on pitching, especially power arms. I don't mean to discount a (Greg) Maddux or a (Tom) Glavine. But power arms are a key component here and were with Montreal and Florida, too."

A trade with Oakland in 2002 brought power arm Jeremy Bonderman. And a deal with Florida in 2003 delivered southpaw starter Nate Robertson.

An 11th-round draft pick in 2002 produced 17-year-old flamethrower Joel Zumaya. A first-round choice in 2004, No. 2 overall, gave the Tigers the services of Justin Verlander, a senior-to-be at Old Dominion.

And the free agent market brought crafty veteran Kenny Rogers to Detroit on December 14, 2005, eight days before Jones returned from Florida. In 2006, they became the American League's All-Star starter and the franchise's career saves king, respectively.

With the arms already in the system and those that were on the way, Leyland decided to leave his home in Pittsburgh and manage for the first time since 1999.

"I knew we had some guys who had a chance to get better quickly in Robertson, Bonderman, and (Mike) Maroth," Leyland said. "I knew we had Zumaya and Verlander in the system. I just didn't know they'd be on the team this year. Then, we went out and signed a guy who made the All-Star team in Kenny—and not just 'cause his team needed a representative. He was 11-3 or something. A lot of people laughed when we made that signing. It looks like a pretty good signing to me."

Let's let Dombrowski explain the rest of his latest construction project, as he did in an exclusive interview in January 2007.

On All-Star catcher Ivan Rodriguez, a free-agent signee before the 2004 season: "'Pudge' was a quality player with Hall of Fame credentials. He's still an All-Star. We did a lot of investigation on how he'd be in an organization that hadn't won in a while. We learned as long as you're committed to winning, he's with you. And we checked his health. We knew he worked very hard and gave himself every chance to be successful."

On trading for Seattle shortstop Carlos Guillen in 2004 after other efforts were foiled: "We had to look at who was available. We tried to sign Rich Aurelia. He was our highest-ranked guy. The Mariners did. So that allowed us to trade for Carlos. We were probably fortunate he'd been injured. When he's on the field for a lot of games, he's a very good player."

On signing free-agent outfielder Magglio Ordonez for 2005: "We took a chance with Magglio. There was some risk with his knee injury. But the doctors said he'd be fine. And we were getting a guy who'd hit .300 with 25 homers and 100 RBIs. Once we felt he'd be healthy, it was an easy decision."

On a loudly ridiculed 2005 trade of reliever Ugueth Urbina for Phillies infielder Placido Polanco, who would go on to be the MVP of the American League Championship Series: "Polanco has always been a solid contributor. You appreciate him more when you see him day in and day out. He knows how to play the game. And when you don't have him in the lineup, you miss him."

On signing Rogers, who had been suspended for shoving a photographer, and Jones, who had been with Detroit once already: "We signed Kenny first and foremost because we thought he could pitch. Then, we thought he could provide leadership. We did check into all the incidents. But Dick Egan spoke very highly of him. With Todd, the big question was the health factor. He threw very well in the second half of 2005 for Florida, when he was 100 percent. We thought he could still be a closer and would give us leadership in the bullpen."

Dave Dombrowski, president, CEO, and general manager, celebrates with Curtis Granderson after the Tigers captured the 2006 American League Divisional Series title. *(Photo by Elsa/Getty Images)*

On hitting the rookie trifecta with center fielder Curtis Granderson, Verlander, and Zumaya: "Granderson was a guy we drafted in 2002 who has continued to improve. He's probably not the ideal leadoff man, because he strikes out quite a bit. But he'll drive the ball. Verlander is a gifted talent with an outstanding arm and outstanding stuff. With the kind of competitiveness he has, he's a No. 1 starter. He won 17 games as a rookie. And he can throw in the mid-90s or higher. Zumaya was a late pick with a great arm and unusual stuff. We converted him from a starter to a reliever. And he projects as a closer in the very near future. People compare him to a young Rich Gossage. I didn't see 'Goose' a lot as a young pitcher. But he probably has that type of arm."

On a July 2006 trade that brought All-Star first baseman Sean Casey from Pittsburgh: "Casey was a proven big-league hitter. He was left-handed. And we needed help at first base. He isn't a big power hitter. But we thought he'd come in, hit close to .300, and be a big help in the clubhouse. He was a good fit."

Every piece to the puzzle didn't fit. The fate of injured closer Troy Percival, a megabucks free agent in November 2004, shows no one is perfect. But Dombrowski's batting average of late is better than Ty Cobb's.

"I think he's a brilliant baseball man," *FSN Detroit* and *Tigers Weekly* contributor Shireen Saski said. "He has an innate sense to surround himself with good people. Yeah, there were guys who didn't pan out. But a lot of guys did."

"Dave gets very little credit for turning this thing around," Detroit talk radio fixture Mark Wilson said. "But it's amazing he kept some of the guys he did. Others would've dumped Brandon Inge. Craig Monroe would've been gone. Nate Robertson would've been history. Dave kept those guys. And Ramon Santiago is back. He's the guy they traded to get Guillen! It's just short of pure genius."

With the right plan and the right man, the seeds of baseball success just had to be nurtured to bloom into victories.

"You know what's funny?" Inge said. "When we lost 119 games, it was almost a matter of, 'It can't get any worse that this!' Or we hoped it wouldn't. But the signings in the off-season showed us they were going in the right direction. We got the players we needed. Then, we went out and got Leyland. That did it! It was just a matter of when."

CHAPTER TWO

The Unquestioned Leader

JIM LEYLAND'S WORDS AND WISDOM

EVEN THE "MARLBORO MAN" NEEDS A HORSE. James Richard Leyland learned that long ago. After earning Manager of the Year honors with Pittsburgh in 1988, '90, and '92 and winning a World Series with Florida in '97, he filled out lineup cards for the salary-strapped, talent-stripped Marlins and went 54-108 the following year.

It wasn't because Leyland forgot how to manage or his players didn't sing "Kumbaya." It was because there weren't enough horses on the roster—a problem he never had in his first season with the Detroit Tigers, 2006 American League Champions.

"I don't believe in chemistry," Leyland said. "Show me a winning team, and I'll show you a good clubhouse. Show me a losing team, and I'll show you a horseshit clubhouse. I've gone to chapel with them and eaten with them, and we've lost 100 games. I've had 'em all hate me and want to punch me in the nose, and we've won 100. I'll take talent. I don't buy all that other stuff."

Welcome to the world and the wisdom of baseball's genius-du-jour, a concept that Leyland rejects even faster than he mocks team chemistry. And that's no great surprise. We're talking about a man's man who refuses to take himself as seriously as his job.

That no-frills, less-phoniness approach began 62 years ago in Perrysburg, Ohio, an hour south of Detroit. If Leyland's dad didn't invent tough love, he practiced it the way his son practiced sports—only in the a.m. and p.m. in days that end in "y".

Young Jim was signed by the Tigers as a catcher in 1963. He hit .222 with four home runs for five teams in six minor-league seasons, then became a coach in 1970 at Montgomery. A year later, Leyland began an 11-year apprenticeship as a manager with Bristol, Clinton, Montgomery, Lakeland, and Evansville.

"I had 18 years of riding the buses," Leyland said before a game last summer. "I never said it was time to go home and find something else to do. I liked it. If I'd have gone home, I probably would've gone back to school and tried to be a high school coach. Instead, I became a professional coach."

It was there in 1978 that he put his indelible imprint on as wild a stallion as the organization had ever signed, ex-Michigan State football/baseball star Kirk Gibson. A great relationship began when Leyland laid the law down to No. 23 as no one had.

"I don't care how much you're making or what you did in football or college baseball," Leyland said as he outlined a rigorous workout schedule. "I'm the manager here. You'll do what I say and do it every day! Is that understood?"

It was understood and appreciated in time. But when Gibson homered to clinch the 1984 World Series, Leyland had finished his third of four years with the White Sox as Tony La Russa's third-base coach. Their lives would be intertwined forever.

Leyland managed the Pittsburgh Pirates from 1986 to 1996. And when *The Sporting News* named him National League Manager of the Year in '98, Leyland's father quickly reminded him that he shared the honor with the Dodgers' Tommy Lasorda. His dad died months later, before Leyland could show him three solo awards and two championship rings.

The Pirates won three straight East Division titles from 1990 to 1992. But with cameras rolling in spring training of '91, Leyland laced into left fielder Barry Bonds, who had just earned his first of seven MVP awards. When Bonds disrespected a coach,

Leyland hollered, "I've kissed your butt for three years! If you don't want to be here, then get your butt off the field!" Today, they have nothing but praise for each other.

In Leyland's first season with the Marlins and president/general manager Dave Dombrowski, Florida finished nine games behind Atlanta in the National League East, then became the youngest expansion team to win it all by edging Cleveland in seven games.

If Leyland thought of getting fat and sassy, 1998 took care of that. When owner Wayne Huizenga ordered Dombrowski to slash payroll, Leyland's horses were out of the barn. And his team was out of the running, plunging from 92 wins to 54.

After one miserable season with Colorado, Leyland knew he'd had enough. He returned home to Pittsburgh and was a different kind of dad. He also worked as a scout for St. Louis from 2000 to 2005, reuniting with his close friend La Russa.

Manager Jim Leyland watches batting practice from inside the Tigers' dugout at Comerica Park before Game 4 of the American League Championship Series on October 14, 2006. *(Photo by Michael Zagaris/MLB Photos via Getty Images)*

"Over the last six years I haven't been offered any managerial jobs," Leyland said. "I've been contacted. I've had discussions with a couple of teams. But I was never offered another job. I was asked if I'd be interested in talking. And I declined."

When the Tigers called, Leyland was ready for one more managerial go-round. On October 4, 2005, he was introduced to the media and didn't know much about Detroit's personnel. He knew enough to think he could win. But no one thought the W's would soar from 71 to 103—95 in the regular season and eight more in the playoffs.

A cross between Bill Parcells and Jack Palance, Leyland was the perfect leader for a franchise that hadn't won 80 games since 1993 and was 43-119 in 2003. That was clear after his rant in 1991. But nothing meant more than an expletive-laced tirade after a 10-2 loss to the Indians on Monday, April 17—getaway day for a nine-game West Coast swing.

"It was the best thing that could've happened to this team when he got on us early in the year," third baseman Brandon Inge said. "It showed how much he cared. And anyone who didn't respond didn't need to be on this ballclub."

A seventh loss in nine games had just dropped Detroit to 7-6. When Leyland's team finished hosting Cleveland again on May 27, the Tigers were 35-15. It was at about that time that Inge said that Leyland could go home. His work was done.

"Inge is right," Leyland said with typical self-deprecation. "I agree with Inge 300 percent. They didn't need me when I got here. And they won't need me when I'm gone. If they can play, they can play. Fortunately, they can play."

Perhaps the best way to understand Leyland and his brutal honesty is to offer a random sampling from three months of interviews in his office. Crusty? Sometimes. Caring? More than you'd guess. And honest? All 525,600 minutes a year.

On his contributions to the turnaround: "I've done nothing. I picked a good staff. And I picked a good job. That pretty much sums it up."

On the fans in Detroit: "Have you looked at the stands lately? I've been in this organization 18 years. This is a baseball town that knows baseball. This isn't the fur coats and all that shit that comes out for the World Series."

On the team's unsung heroes: "We've got scouts and front-office people who work their asses off and never get recognized. I feel bad for them. I've been one of them. They work like dogs for a little money and no credit. And they've done a helluva job."

On his relationship with Dombrowski: "I've got a great boss. He lets me manage the team down here. He doesn't interfere. He gives me the players and says, 'Here they are. You manage them.' That's all you can ask for. We're the best of friends. Sometimes that makes it hard. It also makes it good."

On second-guessing from bosses: "I wouldn't be here. When people say I want to be involved in every piece of the organization, that's not true at all. But I tell people what I think. If my boss asks me, 'What do I need to do?' I give my opinion. That's why he hired me. If you don't want my opinion, don't hire me! Get somebody else."

On dealing with defeat: "You don't get long to celebrate wins, and you don't sit long after losses. I tip my hat to the opposing team. But you can't tip your hat every night and say, 'He pitched a good game.' Sooner or later you have to beat some good pitchers if you want to win anything."

On rally caps and superstitions: "I don't pay attention to that shit. 'Gum Time'—what the hell is that? But they all do it. And I want them to have fun, as long as it doesn't show up the other team. It's not prison. Just be professional at all times."

On home run demonstrations: "Do I like them? No. But I want to refresh everyone's memory. This isn't something new. Babe Ruth did it all the time. He took his hat and waved it around and all that stuff. If a guy hits a grand slam, that's all right. But I don't want Olan Mills coming out there, taking his picture."

On arguing with umpires: "It's part of the game. But the poor bastards call 240 pitches. They're not going to get 'em all right.

It's unbelievable how good they are if you see the replays. I don't go out if it's a safe-out call. It's a waste of time. And I don't believe in getting thrown out to motivate my team. If I have to do that, I should go home. The only problem I have is with arrogant umpires, guys looking for trouble."

On bandwagon support: "The writers are on the bandwagon, too. They were horseshit last year, because the team was horseshit. You can't be good unless we're good. Was it fun covering the team last year? Well, answer the question! You did your job, but was it fun to come to the ballpark to watch a team that was getting its ass beat every night? That's the same way it is for a manager or anyone else. It's the same way for the fans. You've gotta give them something to cheer about. I don't blame 'em."

On evaluating hitters: "I'm a big slugging-percentage guy, not that on-base shit. A lot of guys can get on base. I want a guy who's gonna knock 'em in."

On the value of switch-hitters: "If switch-hitters can hit, it's good. If they can't, it ain't worth a shit."

On disappointing the fans: "I used to get hate mail that said, 'Sonuvabitch! I was coming to three games this year, and you didn't play VanSlyke!' Today, people will say, 'Damn it! Pudge isn't in there! Polanco's not in there! Ordonez isn't in there! What the hell are you doing?' That's why I haven't looked at my mail lately. Once in a while, someone will stop you in public. And I understand it a little bit. If you've got a six-year-old and Pudge is his favorite player, that's tough."

On dealing with the press: "I've been ripped. That's just the way it is. You learn in our business you don't get too excited about a good story or too upset about a bad one. A wrong story? I have no respect for anybody who does that. And someone who lies, I won't talk to. Now, if somebody says, 'You're a horseshit manager!' I don't care about that. I respect people who do their jobs. I know the media has a tough one."

On being his toughest critic: "And at the end of the season, when I go in the bathroom to take my last shower, I say, 'Did I do a good job or a bad job?' To be honest, twice I've said, 'I stunk! I was horseshit.' And that's not a good feeling. I won't tell you which years. I don't want the general manager to know, because I got rehired."

And not by Philip Morris, Inc., as a corporate spokesman, though it could have paid Leyland in Marlboros. He has been hired and rehired because he knows baseball, knows people, and knows better than to be something he's not.

"With no disrespect to Alan Trammell and his staff, who were dealt a difficult hand, Jim Leyland is a better fit for this team," Tigers TV play-by-play man Mario Impemba said. "He knows how to handle personalities and commands instant respect."

Leyland isn't perfect. And if an opponent wanted an edge on the Tigers in a crucial series, a tobacco strike would be a good place to start.

"It's funny, because I remember Opening Day in Kansas City," Impemba said. "Jim said, 'I promised my daughter I'd stop smoking by midnight tonight.' It was about three o'clock in the afternoon. And he said, 'I need to go through seven packs right now.' But he's in better shape than people think."

That was one of the few promises that Leyland hasn't kept. But let's hear from players, past and present, and another high-profile friend.

"He's a General Patton-type guy," former star and team vice president Willie Horton said. "He has passion but knows how to spank your butt. The more he's around you, the more you believe. Even Dmitri Young saw that. He knew being let go was best for him. He had to get his life together. But no one knows he called the day before the World Series. He said, 'Be sure to tell Leyland good luck. And tell the boys downstairs to win it all.'"

"People who aren't around him don't see how much fun he's actually having and how easy he is to play for," closer Todd Jones said. "If you prepare and play hard and get beat, he's okay. If you're not ready, he's going to have issues."

"'Leylandball' is all about preparation and focus," center fielder Curtis Granderson said. "You just have to trust yourself and trust in your teammates."

"I knew Jim in Florida and in Pittsburgh, too," Hall of Fame golfer Chi-Chi Rodriguez said. "He has always been a winner, regardless of what the standings say. He manages by feel. He might lose a game by leaving a young man in, but the return on that trust is great. He knows which buttons to push. Last night, he went to the mound and told Jones to walk the guy. Instead, he threw a perfect pitch and struck the guy out. He has a much better sense of humor than most people see."

If he'd gone to the Yankees and had a different boss, he could've been Joe Torre. Instead, he's back home with Detroit—a Notre Dame fan and a staunch family man who walks to the ballpark and sleeps in his office. Leyland loves his work that much. And, yes, it is work.

His record doesn't match his reputation—1,164 wins, 1,198 losses, .493 winning percentage. But numbers don't begin to tell his story. As much as any leader of men ever could, Leyland understood why Woody Hayes' autobiography was titled *You Win with People*.

There's a tunnel that leads to the batting cages at Comerica Park. A sign there reads, "If tomorrow you could not play, how hard would you play today?" The attribution says "Anonymous" but could've read "Jim Leyland." Those words reflect what the 2006 Tigers were all about.

Manager of the Year? Never in doubt. Man of the Year? His dad would be proud.

CHAPTER THREE

The Recharged Battery

KENNY ROGERS AND "PUDGE" RODRIGUEZ

IT'S STILL A WINNING COMBINATION—something to contribute and something to prove. With ageless athletes and fierce competitors like Kenny Rogers and "Pudge" Rodriguez, the result for the Tigers in 2006 was the best battery since the alkaline.

They didn't have to look alike or talk alike. All they had to do was think alike at game time, especially under pressure. But Rogers, a left-handed pitcher from the south, and Rodriguez, a right-handed catcher from the Caribbean, have more in common than you might imagine.

They both spent the bulk of their careers—12 seasons—with Texas. They both have enough Gold Gloves to start a sporting goods store. And they both earned an American League Championship ring to go with their World Series jewelry—pre-issued by the Yankees and Marlins, respectively.

"The Gambler" is seven years older than "I-Rod," 42 to 35 after both celebrated birthdays in November. But Rodriguez has 70 more homers than Rogers has victories, not counting a postseason showing for the aged.

So let's start with the first one to sign with the Tigers—Ivan Rodriguez Torres. As a youth in Vega Baja, Puerto Rico, he was often compared to 2000 Hall of Fame catcher Carlton "Pudge" Fisk, though Rodriguez remains five inches shorter.

As good as Fisk was, and he was one of the best ever, Rodriguez has a chance to be better, if he isn't already. In 24 seasons with the Sox (Red and White), Fisk hit 376 homers, drove in 1,330 runs, and batted .269. He scored 1,276 runs, stole 128 bases, won one Gold Glove, and finished third in the MVP race in 1983.

Or, if you prefer, let's take a look at Cincinnati's Johnny Bench, generally considered to be the gold standard for backstops with 10 Gold Gloves. In 17 seasons, the two-time National League MVP hit 389 homers, drove in 1,376 runs, and batted .267. Bench scored 1,091 runs and stole 68 bases.

Nice numbers, but Rodriguez can blow by them all if he plays five more years and stays injury-free. In 16 seasons he has 277 homers, 1,119 RBIs, and a .304 batting average. Rodriguez has scored 1,159 runs and stolen 112 bases. Most impressively, the 1999 MVP owns a record 12 Gold Gloves.

Cooperstown, make room for the only Hall of Fame lock the Tigers have had since broadcaster Ernie Harwell was enshrined in 2002.

"He should be a cinch," Harwell said of "the other Rodriguez." "He has enough longevity now. He has all those Gold Gloves. And he may be the best defensive catcher of all time. Johnny Bench used to be the measuring stick on offense and defense. But 'Pudge' can throw with anyone. And he's a better hitter for average than Bench."

When he debuted with the Rangers on June 20, 1991, Rodriguez became the youngest player to catch in a major-league game (19 years, six months, 20 days). And with more power than anyone ever thought possible, his '99 season—116 runs, 199 hits, 35 homers, 113 RBIs, a .332 average, and 25 steals—defied description.

Rodriguez hit a career-high .347 in 2000 and batted .300 or better for the eighth straight time in 2002, his last year in Arlington. After stopping in Florida just long enough to win a

One of the most prominent catchers in baseball, Detroit's Ivan "Pudge" Rodriguez signed with Detroit in 2004. *(Photo by Ed Wolfstein/Icon SMI)*

world title in 2003, Rodriguez was the key free agent for Detroit following its 119-loss nightmare.

"I felt he was a little long in the tooth when the Tigers got him," Harwell said of the 32-year-old. "I was very close to Steve Boros in the Detroit front office, and Steve told me, 'I don't think we're going to sign him. His back is bad.' … I guess he got a physical and showed them his back wasn't as bad as they thought."

His first season with the Tigers was everything President Dave Dombrowski envisioned when he negotiated a four-year, $40 million deal. Rodriguez began his stay in Detroit with 19 homers, 86 RBIs, and a .334 average in a pitcher's park. Add an 11th Gold Glove, and it's not hard to see how his team went from 43 wins to 72.

Or was it his team? In many ways it was supposed to be. But whatever went right in a 29-win upgrade disappeared the following year, a 71-91 sleepwalk. After showing up 22 pounds lighter, Rodriguez wasn't nearly as happy or productive in the final year under Alan Trammell's laissez-faire leadership.

The highlights? A .333 batting average in April, a 57-game errorless streak, a 12th All-Star appearance and a runner-up finish behind Phillies right-fielder Bobby Abreu in the Century 21 Home Run Derby on July 11 at Comerica Park. His rounds of seven, eight, and five homers seemed to tell everyone, "Hey, I can can still hit the longball!"

But Rodriguez's regular-season numbers fell to 14 homers, 50 RBIs, and a .276 average. He didn't win the Gold Glove. And he was fined a game check—$52,000—for showing up late in Kansas City. When Trammell wouldn't approve a trip to Colombia during a four-game suspension, Rodriguez went over his head and went anyway.

From that point forward, or backward in many ways, their relationship soured to lemon-grove levels. Coach Juan Samuel had to intervene once when tempers rose much higher than the Tigers ever did in the standings.

It might not be fair to say that Rodriguez alone got Trammell fired. Many believe his departure from Comerica Park was merely a matter of time. It is accurate that, for the Tigers to be better than a .500 team in 2006, let alone a pennant contender, Trammell's replacement had to establish a working relationship with his best-known player.

Jim Leyland did so immediately, just as he had with Kirk Gibson in the Detroit farm system and with Barry Bonds in a long, successful run at Pittsburgh. By wiping the slate clean, then wiping away any doubt about who was in charge, the seeds of trust were sown.

Both men had World Series rings from the Marlins. Both knew how the game should be played. And both were catchers, even if Leyland's 1,221 at-bats as a pro were with Cocoa, Lakeland, Jamestown, Rocky Mount, and Montgomery.

Leyland gave Rodriguez his space. Rodriguez gave respect in return. Together, they led the 2006 Tigers to heights their mothers wouldn't have imagined. Leyland pushed all the right buttons with an energized team. Rodriguez did his part with a stunning staff of pitchers.

It spoke volumes that he played in 136 games, his second-busiest workload since '99. A .300 batting average, his 10th time at that level, and a 13th All-Star appearance were other signs of a renewed focus. But another Gold Glove was the greatest individual prize. And an American League title meant much more than that.

Rodriguez had just two errors in 801 chances and probably should have handled every ball in front of the mound in an error-filled World Series. With help from pitchers who held runners close, he threw out a major-league-best 45.7 percent of would-be base-stealers. Rodriguez went nearly two months without allowing a swipe, a performance Leyland hadn't seen in ages.

"Not since I caught in Rocky Mount in 1966," he said with a deadpan delivery. "No, I stunk. I'm kidding. I've never seen anything like 'Pudge.' But you're talking about a superstar and a future Hall of Famer.

"Hey, you don't know how much stress that takes off a manager. People don't even notice it. But that's a helluva weapon when people don't even try to run. I was blessed in Florida with Charles Johnson in '97 when we won the World Series. They didn't try to run on him, either."

Only 46 runners tested Rodriguez, and 21 wished they had struck out. It would have saved them the effort and embarrassment. But what other catcher has played with Rodriguez's swagger or commissioned a one-ton, bronze statue of himself to crouch in the backyard of his Miami Beach mansion?

If you ask another Rodriguez, Hall of Fame golfer and good friend Chi-Chi, none of that brilliance was a great surprise for a world-class athlete, regardless of sport.

"It'd be easier for him to play on the PGA Tour than for me to hit a major-league fastball," Chi-Chi said. "If he dedicated himself to golf, he could be one of the best in the world. I mean, he hits the ball 350 yards. He just doesn't play enough. He loves baseball and really works at it. He does about 48 miles a day on the bike, six or seven days a week. And there's no doubt in my mind that he's their most valuable player."

Shortstop Carlos Guillen won that award—and deservedly so. But Tigers TV play-by-play voice Mario Impemba cast a vote for Rodriguez in the season's last week, citing just the kind of team-first attitude that was missing in 2005.

"'Pudge' is a guy you have to watch every day to appreciate," Impemba said. "When Placido Polanco separated his shoulder on that diving catch in Boston, the Tigers had no one to play second base. But 'Pudge,' who'd never done anything but catch before this year, said, 'I'll play second!' He didn't want to embarrass himself at Fenway Park. But he went out there, caught a pop in foul territory and helped his team win. He'll bat sixth in the lineup or first in the lineup. 'Pudge' is their MVP."

He also played first base and looked like a natural—albeit a short one. But that was better than the short fuse he played with the previous year.

"I just don't think he respected 'Tram' as a manager," Impemba added. "'Pudge' is a pretty savvy guy, no matter how he speaks English. But maybe he got a little juvenile. That happens in life. He just wasn't willing to go to war with him. He is for Jim Leyland. If Jim told him to run naked and slam himself into the Houston-Milwaukee score on the scoreboard, he'd do it."

Kenneth Scott Rogers has hung more than his share of zeroes on major-league scoreboards for 18 seasons. The son of a strawberry farmer was a prep outfielder in Plant City, Florida, when he signed with the Texas organization at age 17 for $1,000. After nearly bowling a perfect game in high school, Rogers became just the 14th man to pitch a perfect game on July 28, 1994, when he turned the Angels' halos into zeroes.

After three stints with the Rangers and one each with the Yankees, Athletics, Mets, and Twins, Rogers signed a two-year deal with Detroit worth $16 million.

"I knew once I met Jim Leyland and Dave Dombrowski that this was the place," Rogers said. "I had a friend I'd known my whole life in (longtime Tigers scout) Dick Egan. When I talked with him a few times and got to know Skip and Dave, that was a strong selling point. They made me a pretty good offer, similar to some other ones. But I wanted to be around people I could trust and who'd trust me to go out and do what I do."

What Rogers did last season was become the only southpaw selected for the 2005 and 2006 All-Star staffs. He started the '06 game for the American League and allowed one run in two innings. Rogers did better than that in the regular season, finishing 17-8 with a 3.84 ERA and winning his fifth Gold Glove in the last seven seasons.

"You see guys with great stuff who don't have the numbers to go with it," he said. "Then, you see guys with average stuff who go out and win. I think there's an intangible there. Some guys have the ability to hang in and not give in. They're not afraid to battle with the weapons they have. They don't all have a 96-mile-an-hour fastball or a nasty slider. I appreciate that, 'cause that's where I am in my career. But I know how to pitch. I know how to set hitters up with what I have. The big thing is the ability to adjust."

At age 41, Rogers was five wins and 0.84 earned runs per game better than he was at 31 with the world champion Yankees. And if New Yorkers thought they knew him as a late-season choker, they might need Heimlich maneuvers after Rogers' postseason run.

Twenty-three innings. Twenty-three zeroes. And it started when Rogers fanned eight Yankees in 7 ⅔ innings of Game 3 in the American League Divisional Series, becoming the oldest starting pitcher to earn his first playoff win. When others would have been in rocking chairs, Rogers rocked as never before.

"I'll be there one day," he said. "Right now, I enjoy the competition at this stage of my career. It's basically a bonus. I never expected to be here this long, if at all. But I know my strengths and try to stick to them. When I do that, I'm pretty successful. When I get out of that box, I have trouble. My big advantage is that I'm pretty consistent."

Consistent enough to pitch 7 ⅓ innings against Oakland in Game 3 of the A.L. Championship Series, allowing two hits and striking out six. And just as steady vs. St. Louis in Game 2 of the World Series. In eight innings of two-hit, one-smudge baseball, Rogers retired 10 in a row and made $8 million seem like a free-agent freebie.

"He had a remarkable year," Harwell said. "I thought he'd help. I never thought he'd be sensational. He got rid of the old canard that he couldn't pitch late in the season. He justified their confidence and really solidified the pitching staff. Yeah, he threw a perfect game with Texas. But a perfect game is like a hole-in-one. You've got to be lucky. So many things can happen. In seven decades of broadcasting, I've never seen one. I've seen a lot of no-hitters and a 30-game winner but never a perfect game. Kenny wasn't perfect in the postseason. But he was awful good."

After wrestling with anger-management issues, including an assault on a cameraman in 2005 that led to a 20-game suspension and a $50,000 fine, Rogers was a model of decorum and a great influence on a young pitching staff.

"I saw the raw version of that tape, and my first reaction was, 'What a monster!'" FSN Detroit's Shireen Saski said. "But I interviewed Kenny two weeks into the season, and he was pleasant, charismatic, polite, and interesting. I sat there mesmerized, thinking, 'Who was that other person I saw?'"

Like Rodriguez, he was a different man in 2006—the person and the performer the Tigers hoped they had signed and then some.

CHAPTER FOUR

The Greatest Tiger of All

CHARTER HALL OF FAMER TY COBB

HE WAS HARD TO LIKE AND HARDER TO BEAT. But Tyrus Raymond Cobb was more than the greatest player in Detroit Tigers history. He was "a genius in spikes," as his plaque at Comerica Park proclaims, and a jackass of giant proportions.

Simply put, "The Georgia Peach" was as sweet a hitter and base-stealer as his sport has ever seen. Too bad his dealings with people were the pits.

When he retired in 1928 after 24 seasons, Cobb held 90 major-league batting and base-running records. Barring a fundamental change in the way the game is played, his .366 lifetime average, three .400 seasons, 12 batting crowns, and 54 steals of home will never be matched.

The best tribute to Cobb's competitive greatness, a unique blend of grit and grace, came in 1936. When the Baseball Hall of Fame was founded in Cooperstown, New York, the inaugural class featured just five megastars: Cobb, Babe Ruth, Honus Wagner, Christy Mathewson, and Walter Johnson.

That was precisely their rank when the votes were tallied. Cobb was named on 222 of the 226 ballots cast. Ruth and Wagner each received 215 votes. Mathewson had 205 and Johnson 189.

Cobb's 98.23-percent approval rating was a record until Tom Seaver was named by 98.8 percent in of the voters in 1992. And *The Sporting News* ranked him third on its list of the 100 greatest players in history.

If Cobb had been around to read that, he certainly would've growled, "Third! ... Who's No. 1? ... Who's No. 2?"

Actually, Cobb was No. 1 or No. 2 in the American League in batting average from 1907 to 1919, a span of 13 seasons in which he never hit less than .350. After a slide to .334 in 1920, he bounced back to finish second for the third and fourth times at .389 and .401 the next two years.

Cobb was No. 1 on the hit lists of most pitchers, too. He also had his share of fisticuffs with fans and umpires. If he wasn't the cruiserweight champion of the world, it wasn't from a lack of trying. No one has been cruisin' for a bruisin' more often than Cobb, the product of a truly dysfunctional family.

His father, William Herschel Cobb, was a college graduate and a teacher/farmer in Royston, Georgia. At age 20, "W.H." married 12-year-old Amanda Chitwood. Ty burst onto the scene just three years later as the oldest of three children.

Targeted for West Point or, at worst, a career in medicine, young Master Cobb had other ideas—strong ones, as you might expect. He'd heard the siren's song of baseball and knew he had to give it a shot. The sport he loved and one household would never be the same.

At 17, Cobb left to try out for the Augusta Tourists of the South Atlantic League. When he was cut just two days into the 1904 season, Cobb joined the Anniston Steelers of the semi-pro Tennessee-Alabama League, recalling his father's parting words, "Don't come home a failure."

Always thinking, Cobb sent a series of self-promoting postcards to legendary sportswriter Grantland Rice. Using different handwriting styles and aliases like "Smith" and "Jones," he finally caught Rice's attention. "There's a young fellow named Cobb who seems to be showing an unusual lot of talent," Rice wrote in the *Atlanta Journal*.

After about three months, Cobb returned to the Tourists and hit just .237 in 35 games. Not surprisingly, he fought over pennies that winter in the first of many salary disputes. But with a new contract for $125 a month, a new manager, and the same bad attitude, Cobb tried again in 1905.

It didn't help that he took a bag of popcorn with him to the outfield one day and dropped a fly ball. Cobb thought he could catch the ball and keep the 'corn. He did neither, much to the consternation of manager George Leidy. But it was Leidy who threw bunting practice to Cobb until he could place the ball within inches of his target.

Eventually, Cobb's ability surfaced. He was leading the league in hitting at .326 when the Tigers called. In his major-league debut on August 30, Cobb doubled in his first at-bat.

Three weeks prior to this date, his world changed forever. Earlier in 1905, Cobb's father began hearing rumors of his wife's infidelity and hatched a plan to catch her in the heat of passion. On August 8, W.H. Cobb said he was leaving town for a few days. Instead, he returned to the house that night with a pistol and tried to enter a window.

Alone and scared, Amanda Cobb heard the noise, picked up a loaded, double-barrel shotgun and blasted W.H. After a pause, she fired again, splattering her husband all over the balcony and giving her son another reason to fight.

"I did it all for my father," Cobb told ghostwriter Al Stump in his autobiography. "They killed him when he was still young. They blew his head off the same (month) I became a major-leaguer. He never got to see me play. Not one game, not an inning. But I knew he was watching me ... and I never let him down. Never!"

Instead, Cobb batted over .320 for 22 straight seasons. There was a gap in his grip, but not in his greatness. He won the Triple Crown in 1909 and hit over .400 in 1911, 1912, and 1922. He stole an astounding 892 bases and ranks second in outfield assists, behind fellow center fielder Tris Speaker.

"The greatness of Ty Cobb was something that had to be seen," first baseman George Sisler said. "And to see him was to remember him forever."

Fellow Hall of Famer "Big Train" Johnson added, "He could do everything better than anyone I ever saw."

Unfortunately, that included picking fights—and in most cases, finishing them. Perhaps his prickly personality was to blame. Maybe his problems were rooted in jealousy. But it didn't take long for Cobb to find trouble the second he got to Detroit.

Though his mother was eventually exonerated in the shooting, opposing players and, yes, some teammates couldn't resist running their mouths, as if Cobb's anguish was a license to taunt. You can imagine the reaction when he found the crown ripped out of his hat and his bats sawed in half.

"If I became a snarling wildcat, it was their fault," Cobb said, tracing his combative nature to September 1905. "It was the most miserable and humiliating experience I've ever been through."

His on-field response was to play with more fury, a near-impossibility in some minds. But Cobb took aggression to new heights. He took two bases on routine singles, tried to steal on almost every pitch, and went from first to third with sharpened spikes on sacrifice bunts.

The *Detroit Free Press* might have described Cobb best with the phrase "daring to the point of dementia."

Off the field, he hated Northerners and seemed to be fighting the Civil War 40 years after it ended. Coupled with a persecution complex, it wasn't a warm and fuzzy environment. A loner by nature, Cobb spent most of his free time at museums, art galleries, and libraries.

He became the team's starting center fielder in 1906 and hit .316 in 98 games. Cobb would never hit that low again. But stoop that low? Ty's your guy. During spring training in 1907, he fought an African-American groundskeeper over the field's condition in Augusta, and choked the man's wife when she tried to intervene.

During a game for the Detroit Tigers, Ty Cobb takes a high slide into the knees of the opposing team's catcher. *(Photo by Pictorial Parade/Getty Images)*

That was the year Cobb nearly quit baseball over his paycheck. After making $2,400 in 1906, he finally forced owner Frank Navin to pay him a whopping $5,000.

Also at that time, Cobb immersed himself in business, big and small, and began a long-term relationship with The Coca-Cola Company. Eventually, he'd own bottling plants in California, Oregon, and Idaho, along with more than 20,000 shares of stock. He also did commercial endorsements about drinking the product between double header games.

Cobb's stinginess was laughable. He collected slivers of soap on the floor of the shower room and took them back to Georgia in the off-season. And when gentlemen sailed their hats onto the field, a Labor Day tradition, Cobb had the groundskeepers collect them for his donkeys to keep the animals out of the sun.

On the field, he was every bit as crafty. When Cobb would hobble away from the bag with an apparent leg injury, he'd often take off and steal a base on the next pitch.

Or, as Philadelphia A's manager Connie Mack told his catcher, Ira Thomas, "Keep a tight hold of that glove of yours, or Cobb will be stealing it before you get out of the park."

To make matters worse for catchers, the Navin Field groundskeepers soaked the area in front of the plate to deaden Cobb's bunts and make it slippery for fielders. The spot became known at "Cobb's Lake." One opponent asked if he needed a fishing license to pull balls out of the water.

Intimidation and fear were Cobb's best friends. When he was tagged out, he'd tell the fielder, "Do that again and I'll cut you to ribbons!" Few dared to see if he was kidding.

He was the only player since 1900 to win a home-run title without hitting a ball over the fence. All nine homers in his 1909 Triple Crown season were inside the park. And his mind games with pitchers were seen in his philosophy at the plate: "Every great batter works on the theory that the pitcher is more afraid of him than he is of the pitcher."

After one brushback from Hub Leonard, Cobb bunted the next offering toward the first baseman, let Leonard outrace him to the bag, then spiked him hard from behind.

If Cobb had sprinted as hard as he could, he might've had one more hit. Instead, he finished with two fewer hits than believed, the correction of a clerical error that counted a 2-for-3 outing twice in 1910. That discovery dropped his hit total from the 4,191 that Pete Rose chased to 4,189. It also changed his season average from .385 to .383 and his career mark from .367 to .366.

His batting title that season was in dispute, since Napoleon Lajoie finished at .384. But Cobb's 12th crown should remain intact. The popular Lajoie trailed Cobb heading into the last day of the season, then registered eight hits in a doubleheader against the St. Louis Browns, including six bunts to a third baseman stationed on the outfield grass and another ball that clearly should've been a throwing error.

"All of St. Louis is up in arms over the deplorable spectacle, conceived in stupidity and executed in jealousy," the *St. Louis Press* wrote.

American League president Ban Johnson kicked Browns manager Jack O'Connor and coach Harry Howell out of the league for life. And the Chalmers Automobile Company gave a new car to both men instead of just the champion.

Cobb didn't wear a uniform number with the Tigers. Such an idea wouldn't catch on until the 1930s. And in 1914, he only suited up 98 times. It seems he had a fight with a Detroit butcher, who'd had a run-in with Mrs. Cobb.

In 1915, he teamed with Bobby Veach and Sam Crawford in a dream outfield. They finished 1-2-3 in hits, RBIs, and total bases. Cobb won the batting title and led the American League with 96 steals, a mark that stood for 47 years until Maury Wills had 104.

Cobb's career runs mark of 2,246 stood for 75 years before Rickey Henderson passed him. And he drove in more than 100 runs seven times, mostly during the dead-ball era. By 1921, he was ready for a new challenge and became a player-manager for six seasons.

There, his disdain for Babe Ruth grew. Cobb would wait for Ruth to pass by and ask, "Does anyone smell anything?" referring to Ruth's lack of hygiene. And Cobb's racial epithets to describe Ruth's facial features and complexion triggered a small riot.

But what would you expect from someone who went into the crowd to fight hecklers and knocked umpire Bobby Evans out cold for half an hour with a sneaky head butt under the stands?

On May 5, 1924, Cobb decided to swing for the fences and collected 16 total bases (three homers, a double, and two singles)—still an American League record.

Cobb also stole home at age 40. A week later he did it again, then raced in from right to snare a line drive and beat a wandering base-runner back to the bag for an unassisted double play—or L9 9U, if you're scoring at home.

In 22 seasons with Detroit, Cobb posted franchise records for at-bats, runs, hits, extra-base hits, total bases, singles, doubles, triples, RBIs, on-base percentage, and steals.

In the Joe Falls and Irwin Cohen classic, *So You Love Tiger Stadium, Too*, we see that Cobb was just as competitive at 61. Before his final at-bat, leading off an Old-Timers Game in Yankee Stadium, Cobb politely asked the catcher, "Would you mind moving back a little bit? I haven't done this for a long time. I don't want to lose control of the bat and hit you with it." A few seconds later he said, "Could you move back just a little more?" When the catcher obliged, Cobb bunted the ball in front of the plate and beat the throw to first for a single—unofficially, hit No. 4,190.

When he died in Atlanta on July 17, 1961, a player the Tigers acquired for $700 was worth a fortune of more than $7 million—Cobb's favorite statistic of all.

A *New York Times* editorial read, "Let it be said that Cobb was the greatest of all ballplayers." Ty would've liked that eulogy, especially coming from Ruth's home for so many seasons. But if life is all about people, maybe it says even more that only two baseball players attended his funeral.

CHAPTER FIVE

The Legendary G-Men

CHARLIE GEHRINGER AND HANK GREENBERG

"THE MECHANICAL MAN" AND "HAMMERIN' HANK" were American League MVPs two years apart. They both were elected to the Baseball Hall of Fame. And the Detroit Tigers retired their numbers—2 and 5—on the same day. Only the statues beyond the stands in left-center field at Comerica Park will wear them now.

But Charlie Gehringer and Hank Greenberg were more than world championship teammates. They were the greatest right side of the infield in baseball history and might've been the top tandem any team has had aside from Babe Ruth and Lou Gehrig.

Gehringer and Greenberg … Greenberg and Gehringer. Where do we begin? Whether we make that decision alphabetically, numerically, or chronologically, the second baseman always comes first. It's the No. 3 hitter, then the cleanup spot.

Charles Leonard Gehringer was arguably the second-best second sacker in history. He's behind Rogers Hornsby, in the neighborhood with Nap Lajoie and Eddie Collins, and ahead of Jackie Robinson and Joe Morgan.

"The Fowlerville Flash" was a career .320 hitter and won the batting title in 1937, his MVP year, with a .371 mark. He also led the league in assists and fielding percentage seven times.

Charlie Gehringer, pictured here in the late 1930s, played his entire baseball career with the Tigers. *(Photo by Bruce Bennett Studios/Getty Images)*

No one ever walked softer and carried a bigger stick than Gehringer, a silent assassin who spent 19 seasons—16 as an everyday player—with his only major-league team. And no wonder he was such a great glove man. For 89 years, he never left the mitten that was Michigan's Lower Peninsula.

"He'd say 'hello' at the start of spring training and 'goodbye' at the end of the season," his first manager, a cantankerous Ty Cobb, said. "The rest of the time he'd let his bat and glove do the talking for him."

Gehringer hit over .300 13 times and had more than 200 hits in seven seasons. He finished with 2,839 hits, including 574 doubles, 146 triples, and 184 home runs. He also swiped 181 bases—not bad for a guy who lettered in basketball but never in baseball at the University of Michigan.

A student of the game who flunked self-promotion, Gehringer twice led the American League in runs and hits and finished No. 1 in doubles, triples, and steals in the same season, 1929. He also had a career-high 404 putouts that year.

But the best measure of his bat control might have come in 1936, when Gehringer had a career-high 641 at-bats, 90 walks, and just 13 strikeouts—roughly one K every two weeks. He hit .354 and had 144 runs, 227 hits, 60 doubles, 12 triples, 15 homers, and 116 RBIs. More home runs than strikeouts? Sounds more like softball than baseball.

"He hits .350 on Opening Day and stays there all season," Yankees pitcher Lefty Gomez said. "All I know is when I'm pitching, he's always on base."

He was always at second base during the first six All-Star Games. From 1933 to 1938, Gehringer played every inning of the Mid-Summer Classic, hitting a record .500 in 20 at-bats. And in three World Series in a seven-year span, he hit .321. Appropriately, when Detroit won it all in 1935, Gehringer hit .375 and handled 39 chances in the field without an error.

The 5-foot-11, 180-pounder choked up on the bat and kept a firm stranglehold on dominance at his position. Throughout the Great Depression, the one thing that never dipped was

Gehringer's performance. He had two streaks of more than 500 consecutive games and played in at least 98 percent of Detroit's games nine times.

Gehringer improved in the Triple Crown categories—batting average, homers, and RBIs—for five straight seasons from 1926 to 1930. Hornsby was the only other player to do that. And when the Tigers held "Charlie Gehringer Day" on August 14, 1929, an odd salute for a 26-year-old, he responded with four hits, a homer, and a steal of home.

When *The Baseball Page* rated his greatest strength and biggest shortcoming, it said, "Consistency" and "Gehringer had no glaring weaknesses." It forgot public speaking and an inability to clone himself.

Gehringer was the team's general manager from 1951 to 1953 and a vice president from 1953 to 1959. Appropriately, he held the first of those jobs when 18-year-old Al Kaline was signed. Gehringer and Kaline had plenty in common and played a combined 41 seasons, all in Detroit. Both Hall of Famers did what they could and believed in help, not hype.

Perhaps Gehringer remembered what happened when he signed with the Detroit organization. In his first year, 1924, he made $3,500 and began with London in the Michigan-Ontario League. When he left for three days for his father's funeral, he returned to find he'd been docked three days' pay.

Despite growing up on a 230-acre farm, Gehringer didn't own a gun and didn't care for hunting. When his teammates wanted to do so, they were strictly on their own. Besides, at holiday time, he was too busy working at J.L. Hudson.

Gehringer worked hard at his craft and became the first player to record a natural cycle—a single, a double, a triple, and a homer, in that order—in 1937. In the field he tried to be less spectacular, as he said in a lengthy interview in Richard Bak's book, *Cobb Would Have Caught It.*

"Infielders are rarely spectacular," Gehringer said. "I've always said infielders don't win games. They save them. It's all mechanical. If you had to stop and think, 'Now, how am I going to field this ball?' it'd be past you. Your reflexes take over. You have to think before the ball is hit. That's where a lot of mistakes are made. You've got to see what the potential is, then say, 'Well, I'm going to throw to this base if I get the ball.' You can't be thinking, 'Gee, what am I going to do tonight after the game?'"

The games ended for Gehringer when he enlisted in the Navy in 1942. And when he died at age 89 in 1993, his passing was barely noted across the nation. If you don't make noise when you're living, it's hard to get attention when you're gone. But at least one national columnist, Shirley Povich of *The Washington Post*, paid tribute with an apology.

Povich had signed off on Robinson's selection as a Dream Team second baseman in *Sports Illustrated*. Three months later, he wanted to retract that choice in a eulogy, "Quiet Greatness."

"Charlie Gehringer deserved more and better," Povich wrote. "At Cooperstown, even in the presence of the Hall of Fame's most famous, his plaque glitters. That (his death) was given the brush-off probably speaks to the new values of the sports media. Television and the sports pages would have screamed the news if Michael Jordan had revealed that he had a slow-growth hangnail."

Henry Benjamin Greenberg grew to be a major sociological force as the first Jewish star in baseball. The American League MVP in 1935 and '40 led the league in home runs and RBIs four times and led both leagues in courage until Robinson joined the Brooklyn Dodgers in 1947.

Greenberg was born in New York City, went to school in the Bronx and turned down the Yankees to attend NYU, in part because they already had a sturdy first baseman—some guy named Gehrig. One year later, Greenberg signed with the Tigers for $9,000.

He had one at-bat with Detroit in 1930 at age 19, then returned from a three-year stint in the minors at 22. The 6-foot-4 Greenberg's first real chance with the Tigers produced a .301 average and 87 RBIs, a hint of what was to come.

In 1934, he hit .339, led the American League with 63 doubles, and ranked third with 139 RBIs and a .600 slugging percentage. But Greenberg did more by not playing one day than he did in his career's best game.

With Detroit leading the league by four games in early September, he had to decide what to do about his religion's High Holy Days. Greenberg elected to play on Rosh Hashanah and hit two home runs against Boston in a 2-1 win. Ten days later he spent Yom Kippur in a synagogue, inspiring this poem by Edgar Guest:

> *Come Yom Kippur—holy fast day wide-world over to the Jew—*
> *And Hank Greenberg to his teaching and the old tradition true*
> *Spent the day among his people and he didn't come to play*
> *Said Murphy to Mulrooney, "We shall lose the game today!*
> *We shall miss him in the infield and shall miss him at the bat,*
> *But he's true to his religion—and I honor him for that!"*

Anti-Semitism couldn't stop "The Baseball Moses" any better than opposing pitchers did.

"Throw him a pork chop! He can't hit that!" the St. Louis Cardinals taunted during the '34 World Series.

The following year, Greenberg hit everything. He led the league with 170 RBIs and a career-high 389 total bases. He also ranked second with 46 doubles, 16 triples, and a .628 slugging percentage.

Greenberg's numbers in 1937 were even better. He drove in 183 runs, the third-highest total in history, while batting .337 with 200 hits. Greenberg hit the first-ever homer into the center-field bleachers at Yankee Stadium. And he ranked second with 40 homers, 59 doubles, a .668 slugging percentage, and 102 walks—not bad in Gehringer's MVP season.

The following year brought a serious challenge to Ruth's hallowed record of 60 home runs. Greenberg homered in four straight at-bats and finished with 58 of them. He was intentionally walked several times toward the end of the season. And many still believe that happened to keep a Jew from holding the most important record in sports.

Who knows how many homers he'd have hit if he hadn't tied for the league lead with 119 walks in 1938? We do know that Greenberg led the league with 144 runs and ranked second with 146 RBIs and a .680 slugging percentage.

We also know that Greenberg went into the White Sox clubhouse to confront manager Jimmy Dykes. And it bothered him that he couldn't buy property in the plush Detroit suburb of Grosse Pointe. But his responses generally came in the form of a long home run and another tour of the bases.

He responded as well as anyone could after a move to the outfield in 1940. Greenberg hit 41 homers and led the league for the third time in six years. He batted .340 and was first in the American League with 150 RBIs, 50 doubles, 384 total bases and a .670 slugging percentage. That made him one of just three players to be named MVP at two positions.

"He was one of the truly great hitters," Yankees hero Joe DiMaggio said. "When I first saw him at bat, he made my eyes pop out."

As World War I approached, Greenberg was first diagnosed with flat feet and classified 4F by the Detroit draft board. Amid rumors that he'd bribed officials, Greenberg passed a second examination and was drafted in late 1940. He was honorably discharged on December 5, 1941, after Congress released all men age 28 or older.

When the Japanese bombed Pearl Harbor two days later, Greenberg re-enlisted in the Army Air Corps, completed Officer Candidate School, and was commissioned as a first lieutenant, serving in the China-Burma-India Theater.

He returned to baseball in the summer of 1945 and was selected to play in the All-Star Game without a single day of spring training. Greenberg homered in his first game back, drove in 60 runs in 78 games, and saved the best for last. His ninth-inning grand slam in the final game of the season gave the Tigers the American League pennant.

After leading the league for the final time with 44 homers and 127 RBIs in 1946, Greenberg became embroiled in a salary dispute and was traded to the Pittsburgh Pirates, where he became the first $100,000 ballplayer. Fittingly, he was also one of the first players to go public and embrace Robinson's arrival. If Greenberg didn't know everything Robinson would face, he knew a lot more than most.

"Class tells," Robinson said. "It sticks out all over Mr. Greenberg."

Greenberg said goodbye after a year in Pittsburgh, only his ninth full season. In a career without interruptions, he would've hit more than 500 homers. Instead, in just eight full seasons with Detroit, he finished with 306 to go with 1,202 RBIs in 1,269 games.

After serving as farm director, general manager, and part owner of the Cleveland Indians, another first for a Jew, Greenberg became part owner of the White Sox, again with Bill Veeck. Blocked by the Dodgers' Walter O'Malley in a bid to own an American League expansion team in Los Angeles, Greenberg became a successful Wall Street investment banker.

At about that time, Dodgers pitcher Sandy Koufax became the second Jewish superstar in baseball. His path to success and acceptance had been blazed by Greenberg.

"I thought he'd be the first Jewish president," attorney Alan Dershowitz said.

Actor Walter Matthau said, "I joined the Beverly Hills Tennis Club to eat lunch with him. I don't even play tennis."

Greenberg died of cancer in 1986 in Beverly Hills, California. Twenty years later, he was saluted on one of four commemorative stamps issued by the U.S. Postal Service. But the greatest tribute is the way his memory lives on in the name of cancer research.

The Michigan Jewish Sports Foundation has held the Hank Greenberg Memorial Golf & Tennis Invitational for nearly 20 years and has generated close to $2 million to battle the disease. All these years and he's still battling to make the world a better place.

CHAPTER SIX

The Face of a Proud Franchise

BONUS BABY-TO-ICON AL KALINE

NO ONE EVER CALLED HIM AL STATLINE. And worshipping fans certainly could have. But for all his accomplishments, Albert William Kaline was known for impeccable style, not just impressive statistics.

For most of his 22 seasons in Briggs/Tiger Stadium, "The Line" was more than a star in right field. He was Sirius, the brightest light in the nighttime sky. And as great as some of his numbers were—and still are half a century later—his numbing consistency and constant class were even more impressive.

The youngest player to win a major-league batting championship became just the 10th man to be inducted into the Baseball Hall of Fame on his first try. But that's what happens when you get 3,007 hits, win 10 Gold Gloves, and play in 18 All-Star Games—all for one fortunate team in a four-sport town.

Thus, it's strange to think that Kaline's career almost ended before it began. He was born on December 19, 1934, in Baltimore, the same city that gave us Babe Ruth. And his father, two uncles, and a grandfather were all semipro catchers. That didn't stop him from contracting osteomyelitis and having two inches of bone removed from his left foot.

Suddenly, the pain was gone—unless you were an opposing pitcher. So it was no surprise that Kaline became a hot commodity in an era with no amateur draft. And if not for the work of one persistent scout, the history of at least two franchises would be dramatically different.

"Ed Katalinas got real close to my family, my father in particular," Kaline remembered late in the 2006 regular season. "He watched me play for three years in high school and told my father not to sign anything until he had a chance to talk with us."

That sales pitch reflected what Katalinas had told Detroit's front office after a 50-104 finish in 1952 and a third of the way through a 60-94 season in 1953—that Kaline, at 6-foot-2 and less than 140 pounds, was better than any outfielder on the major-league roster.

"There were a lot of teams after me," Kaline said. "Some of them offered more money than the Tigers. But we wanted to go to a team I might have a chance to make. After going over the rosters and finding out who their better outfielders were in the minors, we decided we'd sign with Detroit because I wanted a chance to play."

He'd go on to play in a franchise-high 2,834 games, 29 more than Ty Cobb. But no one knew what a bargain he'd be when the Tigers signed him for $35,000—some deferred. And it was not the last time Kaline would leave money on the table in negotiations.

With anyone else, the dollar difference of the offers alone might've put him in hitter-friendly Fenway Park opposite Boston left fielders and Hall of Famers Ted Williams and Carl Yastrzemski.

"The most money was offered by the Red Sox and the Philadelphia Phillies," Kaline said. "Both offered me a lot more money than the Tigers. But both teams were good at the time and had a lot of good outfielders. I really didn't think I'd get a chance for two years. And I had to be in the majors that long because I signed a bonus contract. So I decided to play with Detroit."

Hours after becoming the first Kaline to earn a high school diploma, he signed what would later become a lifetime contract.

Since the franchise's start, one of Detroit's most beloved players has been outfielder Al Kaline. *(Photo by Photo File/MLB Photos via Getty Images)*

The money all went to his parents to pay for his mother's eye operation and pay off their mortgage.

Without spending a day in the minors, Kaline debuted in right field on June 25, 1953. He was 18 years, six months and six days old at the time—appropriate for a player who soon became known as "Six" to his teammates. Fittingly, No. 6 became the first of five numbers that the Tigers have retired.

"A big part of it was just having a chance to play," Kaline said. "I'd had a lot of experience playing amateur baseball. I'd played four years of semipro ball against former pros who'd been good enough to sign contracts. But coming to a team that was in last place at the time meant a young kid had a chance to play."

Rookie highlights included a single off the legendary Satchel Paige and the first four of his franchise-high 399 home runs. But it was a tough transition for a teenager living in Detroit's Wolverine Hotel and wearing his only suit day after day. After the team's many afternoon games, he watched movies and wandered the streets alone.

But no less a judge of talent than Williams, the game's last .400 hitter, saw something special in Kaline and suggested he build his wrists by squeezing baseballs as hard as he could. One year later, a minor who weighed in at 157 pounds was the biggest story in the majors.

On April 17, 1955, Kaline hit three homers against Kansas City, including two in one inning. It was the first time a player had done so since Joe DiMaggio in 1936. And with a year Williams or DiMaggio gladly would've taken, Kaline's .340 average, 27 homers, and 102 RBIs left him second to Yogi Berra in MVP balloting.

When Kaline won his batting title at age 20, he was one day younger than Cobb had been in 1907. That comparison was almost as unfair as it was unhealthy. History says there was only one Cobb, winner of 12 batting titles. But in 1955, the first of his 13 straight All-Star seasons, there was only one Kaline, too.

"It was just one of those magical years," he said with his usual modesty. "I never struck out very much, I put the ball in play, and I got quite a few infield hits. I was a real thin guy, so pitchers thought they could overpower me. They challenged me a little more than they should've. But I took advantage of my opportunity. The only thing I'd ever wanted to do was to play baseball."

He played the game the way it was supposed to be played and was as elegant as he was excellent in his prime. And though he was never considered a great slugger, a game that was never finished in 1958 cost Kaline a 400th home run.

"The first ballgame I ever covered, the Tigers were playing the White Sox," longtime *Detroit News* writer Jerry Green said. "Kaline hit a homer to right in the fourth inning. Then, it started to rain. They never finished the game, so it wasn't official. With that one, he would've hit 400. I told him that story many years later, and Al said, 'I don't remember it.' I said, 'I do!' and had the clipping to show him—one paragraph for the Associated Press."

Not enough paragraphs have been written about Kaline's best power year. By May 26, 1962, he was batting .340 with 13 home runs and 38 RBIs. On a diving catch for the final out in a win at New York, Kaline fractured his collarbone and missed nearly two months. He still hit 29 homers and drove in 94 runs in 100 games.

The following year he batted .312, hit 27 homers, drove in 101 runs, and was brilliant in right. He finished second to Yankees catcher Elston Howard in the MVP race, but was named the American League Player of the Year by *The Sporting News* for the second time.

"There have been a lot of great defensive players," Baltimore third baseman and Gold Glove vacuum Brooks Robinson said. "The fella who could do everything was Al Kaline. He was just the epitome of what a great outfielder is all about—great speed, catches the ball, and throws the ball real well."

He set a record for American League outfielders, with 242 errorless games in a row. And if you saw him chase a shot down the line, play the ball off the wall, whirl and fire a strike to nail another stunned runner, you know all about "Kaline's Corner." If not, you can always check the sign marking that spot at Comerica Park.

Before Willie Horton cracked Detroit's outfield in the mid-1960s, he wisely studied Kaline at every opportunity. Ironically, it was Horton, not Kaline, who had the key defensive play for the Tigers in the 1968 World Series, retiring Lou Brock on a throw to the plate to survive in Game 5.

Meanwhile, it was Kaline who had the game-winning hit, a two-run single, to keep the Tigers alive that day. And after a Game 7 win in St. Louis, Kaline's numbers—a .379 average, two homers, and eight RBIs—silenced his few remaining critics.

"Al has always been quiet," Horton said. "Coming up, I watched him a lot. If you went to him, he'd speak from the heart. He had quiet leadership. I saw how he went about his business and prepared for games. I watched him in batting practice. I guess I was just a nosy kid. But I watched him till he got tired of me. That's how you learn."

Very few players pick his brain at the batting cage these days, something that disappoints Kaline in his role as special assistant to the president. It's clear they could learn patience at the plate from a player with 1,277 career walks, the most in club history.

"I wasn't what you'd call a home-run hitter, so I really didn't have a long swing," Kaline said. "Most of the guys who strike out today have long swings and get fooled on a lot of pitches. I was more of a short-swing, put-the-ball-in-play type of player. Every once in a while, I'd hit a home run. But that wasn't my main goal."

He still hit 20 or more homers nine times and had 226 of them at Briggs/Tiger Stadium, another record. If Kaline hadn't started with a season few mortals could match or had been more of a self-promoter, he would've been an even bigger star—a tough assignment for a player with 88.31-percent Hall of Fame approval.

"I wasn't really concerned about recognition," Kaline said. "I was glad I played in Detroit. It was a great town for me—not too big and not too small. But anybody who plays the game wants to play in the big game. You want to know, 'How will I respond?' I did pretty well in All-Star Games (batting .324 and fielding 1.000). And in '68, I got my chance in the Series and didn't fall flat on my face. I thought my time was running out after 16 years."

His time continued for another six years, including a near miss in the 1972 American League Championship Series. "Mr. Perfection," as manager Billy Martin called him, homered in Game 1 and led the Tigers with five hits in five games.

The following year, Kaline became the third recipient of the Roberto Clemente Award for commitment to his community and value of others. Some still smirk, wondering if Kaline valued himself enough. After all, how many people ever turn down a pay raise?

Ruth surely didn't. When asked why he made more money than the president, he quickly answered, "I had a better year." Kaline had plenty of good ones, too, but not enough as he saw it. Let's hear the story from the man who said, "Thanks! … But no thanks. … Maybe next season."

"I was making $96,000 a year in '71, and the media wanted me to be the first $100,000 player here," Kaline said. "That was the ultimate number back then. Anybody who made $100,000 was supposed to be a superstar, a Mantle, or a guy of that stature.

"I hadn't really had a good year. And the team sent me a contract for the same amount of money, then called and said, 'No, we want to give you the extra $4,000.' I said, 'Nah, I didn't have that good a year. And you initially wanted to give me the same contract.' So I turned down the extra $4,000, which was a lot of money back then.

"You didn't get many raises more than $4,000 in those days. I led the league in 1955 and got a $5,000 raise. People made a big deal of it. But I have to live with myself. And I know baseball. It's all I ever wanted to do. I wasn't going to try to gouge somebody because I had been around for a while."

He wound up getting the $100,000 contract in 1972. But for those who say Kaline wouldn't have left the Tigers if he'd played at the peak of the free-agent era, don't be so sure.

"I don't know about that," Kaline said with a laugh. "I can turn down $4,000. But I don't know if I could turn down $4 million dollars from some club!"

Maybe he wouldn't have had to do that. Maybe his numbers and popularity would've made him the highest paid Tiger in history. Teams have certainly spent money for worse reasons than to reward performances like Kaline's.

"Maybe they would've paid me," he said. "That's hindsight. I hope I've meant enough to them that they would. Again, the money issue has never been big with me. I always thought that money was the root of all evil anyway. People do terrible things when money is involved. I've always thought, if you do something just for the money, you're not doing the right thing. I played this game because I loved it. And it was good to me financially. But that wasn't the reason I played."

He played as an icon for all that was good about the game and positive about his adopted city and state. He played hard and long, becoming the 12th player to get 3,000 hits after doubling off Dave McNally on September 24, 1974.

Despite a broken cheekbone in 1959, the aforementioned collarbone in 1962, rib injuries in 1965 and 1973, foot surgery in 1965, a broken finger in 1967, and the broken arm a year later, Kaline set another American League record by playing 100 or more games in 20 seasons.

He worked at his craft and played like a child. Now, at age 72, Kaline is beginning his 55th year as a Tiger, including 26 in the broadcast booth. And if he'd line a single to left or keep a runner from trying for two, I'd pay the $4,000 myself to see it happen one more time.

CHAPTER SEVEN

The Barrier Busters

DETROIT, WILLIE HORTON, AND RACIAL PIONEERS

MORE THAN 11 YEARS after Jackie Robinson broke the color barrier in Major League Baseball in 1947, the Detroit Tigers became the next-to-last team to integrate, beating only the Boston Red Sox.

On June 6, 1958, Osvaldo Jose Virgil Pichardo—Ozzie Virgil, to most of us—suited up for the Tigers and went 1-for-5 in a win at Washington. Eleven days later, he made his Motor City debut at third base, drew a standing ovation at a predominantly white Briggs Stadium to start the game, then went 5-for-5 in another win over the Senators.

Acquired in an off-season trade with the Giants, Virgil had played in the minor leagues with Detroit pitchers Hank Aguirre and Jim Bunning and was accepted by most of his teammates. The same couldn't be said for blacks in Metro Detroit, who saw him in a different light—as the Dominican Republic's first player in the majors, not as one of their own.

The first African-American Tiger was Hall of Fame outfielder Larry Doby, the first black player in the American League. Acquired in an off-season trade with the White Sox in 1959, Doby played 18 games for Detroit and had 12 hits and four RBIs in the last year of a classy career.

It took another two years for the Tigers to embrace African Americans as everyday players. But before second baseman Jake Wood and center fielder Billy Bruton could bat one and two in the order in 1961, a history of racist policies had to disappear.

The problem had been clear as far back as 1923. While Norman "Turkey" Stearnes and the Detroit Stars of the Negro National League thrilled minority fans and occasionally outdrew the Tigers, Stearnes worked at Briggs Manufacturing Company, of all places. He couldn't have played for Walter Briggs' team for another 35 years.

Openly embracing bigotry with the slogan "No jigs for Briggs," Detroit was long known as a bastion of baseball bigotry. That was never clearer than on June 13, 1924, 11 years before Frank Navin died and Briggs bought the team. When Ty Cobb triggered a brawl by repeatedly calling archenemy Babe Ruth "Nigger," more than 1,000 fans joined in the mayhem before police restored order.

When Briggs died in 1952, his family sold the Tigers four years later to Fred Knorr, a staunch supporter of integration. Knorr quickly contributed $75,000 to sign and develop 17 black players in the farm system.

Long after the Negro Leagues signed two white players in 1950, Detroit's farm system finally produced a black star, which brings us to the tale of homegrown hero Willie Wattison Horton.

"Growing up in the Jeffries Projects just blocks away, I used to play this game, Strikeout, against the walls of the stadium," Horton said. "We used to hide in the dumpster till the gates opened, then jump the fence and slip in. One time I got caught. And of all people, it was Rocky Colavito who got me out of trouble—him and the guy with the big ears ... ummm ... Don Mossi!"

Colavito was Cleveland's left fielder in those days, a heartthrob hero and future American League home-run king. Little did Horton or anyone else know "The Rock" would be dealt to Detroit in 1960 for batting champion Harvey Kuenn,

Homegrown hero Willie Horton poses for a portrait.
(Photo by Louis Requena/MLB Photos via Getty Images)

handing the job to the scared kid and would-be catcher he'd rescued.

"I was about 12 years old," Horton said. "Rocky told the officer, 'I'll take it from here,' then got me my first job with the visiting clubhouse guy, Rip Collins. Rocky was my hero after that. Taking over for him was a dream come true."

Most of Horton's dreams came true. He hit a tape-measure homer for Detroit Northwestern High in the 1959 city championship game at Briggs Stadium. He helped the Tigers win a World Series nine years later with his offense AND defense. And he became an inspiration to kids and grown-ups in the city's black community.

"That ball I hit when I was a freshman in high school bounced off the light tower in right-center," Horton said. "The umpire had to tell me to run. I was scared. I'd never seen a ball hit like that. Finally, he told me, 'Son, you have to run around the bases to get a home run.'"

Horton figured that out in a hurry. And it was a good thing he did, since he hit 325 homers for six American League teams, including 262 with Detroit, the fourth-most in franchise history. But his development was as unique as his hands-high, weight-back batting stance.

"Nobody ever told me how to hold a bat or stand or anything like that," Horton said. "When I was in the projects and they were building the Lodge Freeway with all that construction, I'd hit bottle caps that would sail all the way across. I used to run home and tell my mom and dad, and Papa didn't believe me. He told me I'd better quit telling so many tales or he was going whip my butt. Mama just said to keep hitting them.

"It was the same way in professional baseball. Gates Brown was a little ahead of me. I was down in Dunedin, Florida, taking batting practice, and said, 'Mr. Brown, what are you trying to do?' He said, 'I'm trying to hit the ball across that field.' I said, 'See that school over there? I can hit that.' He said, 'You can't hit that!' So I picked the ball up and hit it. It was just something that was natural."

So was Horton's relationship with "The Gator." William James Brown, who served a brief stint in the Ohio State Reformatory for burglary, showed exactly what someone can do with a second chance, great ability, and good intentions. He also showed Horton more about hitting than most batting coaches teach an entire team.

Brown's debut was delayed a bit when the manager who told him he'd play the next day, Bob Scheffing, was fired in 1963. But in 13 seasons, no one ever made more of his opportunities. Brown set American League records with 107 pinch hits and 16 homers. And his 74 pinch-hit RBIs don't begin to tell the story.

Brown hated spring training so much he'd splash water all over the front of his uniform so the coaches would think he'd sweated profusely. The coup de gras? He'd follow those non-workouts with rubdowns from trainer Bill Behm.

"No one will ever know how many games he affected," said starting pitcher Earl Wilson, a key acquisition from Boston in 1966 and the lone black to start a World Series game for Detroit. "Other managers knew Gates was in the dugout and arranged their strategy to keep him off the field."

Nothing could keep Horton off the field for long. The youngest of Clinton and Lillian Horton's 21 children signed a professional baseball contract before he had a high school diploma, a voter registration card, or the right to have a postgame beer.

"I was 17 years old," Horton said. "I signed half a year before I finished high school down in Florida. I was a hardship case, so I could help my mom and dad. My dad was on disability. And I had an opportunity to do something for them. Actually, the Tigers tried to sign me the year before, but the law wouldn't let them."

Horton's bonus bought his parents a home that was once owned by Henry Ford's family, plus a 10-year pension. Willie lived off an allowance of $50 every two weeks when his dad sold a car that was part of that deal. But it was a short trip from heaven to hell.

His first big-league at-bat in September 1963 was, of course, a game-tying homer to left off Hall of Famer Robin Roberts. That swing led to his father's arrest. Seated in his favorite spot in the bleachers, Clinton Horton jumped up and down and yelled, "That's my son! That's my son!" When no one believed him, a fight ensued. His son just smiled when he heard the story.

A starting spot in left was Horton's for the taking in 1965. On New Year's morning, though, none of that mattered. He was awakened in Puerto Rico by a group of players, including high school teammate Alex Johnson and Hall of Famer/humanitarian Roberto Clemente, with the worst news imaginable.

His parents, his brother, Billy, and two nephews were sardines in a car that hit the back of a salt truck in blizzard conditions on I-94, near Albion. Clinton Horton died instantly. Lillian and Billy were in critical condition.

It took a half-day for Horton to get back to Detroit, where Brown met him at Metro Airport. Long before they could complete a three-hour slalom halfway across the state, Lillian Horton died, too.

That spring in Lakeland, Horton carried the weight of the world on his massive shoulders. It didn't help that race relations in the South were still horrendous, and attitudes in the supposedly enlightened North weren't much better beneath the surface.

As late as 1962, Tiger starters like Wood and Bruton weren't allowed to stay at the team's Florida headquarters, the Regency Hotel. They had to find rooms with black families in the area or stay in bunks at Tigertown, despite the objections of John Fetzer and Jim Campbell.

"That's just the way life is," Horton said. "My dad told me, 'You can't rush things.' When Mr. Fetzer bought the team and brought Mr. Campbell in to run the show, I remember him saying he respected what I was doing, but he couldn't change it all at one time. It was going to take some time. I learned you can't do it all in one night. It's the same way in other walks of life, whether it's the police department or anything else. I'm just blessed that the good Lord kept me patient."

People on both sides of the racial divide tested Horton's patience in the late 1960s. When the Detroit riots erupted at 12th Street and Clairmount on Sunday, July 23, 1967, he had no idea why black smoke billowed high above the left-field roof. But when a doubleheader with the Yankees ended, he was told to leave Tiger Stadium immediately. Instead of heading home, he headed … HOME … and drove to the fires in full uniform in a futile attempt to quell the violence.

"I got totally involved," Horton said. "Something just took me there, where I used to deliver the *Michigan Chronicle*. These were my people. I stood on top of my car and pleaded for them to stop. They said, 'Go home, Willie! This isn't about you.' I learned from all the heartache."

The fires burned for five days. When they stopped, 43 people were dead. Another 1,189 were injured. More than 400 homes were burned. And more than 2,500 businesses were destroyed or looted.

Meanwhile, Horton's life was nowhere near as peaceful as it seemed. He kept his emotions bottled up amid hate mail and death threats. One man was arrested for threatening his family. Special security was hired to protect his kids en route to school.

"I guess they weren't ready for a black star," Horton said. "Maybe they were ready for a regular ballplayer, but not a star. Internally, it was just as bad. We had some people in our own organization telling other teams how to pitch to me. I remember Yogi Berra telling me, 'That won't matter. You see the ball, and you hit it.'

"But I had a lot of uncomfortable things that I went through. They made a better man and a better person out of me. That's the way I live my life and why I wrote my own book, *The People's Champion*. I helped make things better, not only in Detroit but in Lakeland."

Horton did that in a way few could have imagined. He walked off the field once to get more black players in the Detroit organization. He didn't make it a federal case. But the people who had to know it knew. Now, everyone does.

"People said I had a problem with Mr. Campbell," Horton said. "I never had a problem with Mr. Campbell or the Detroit Tigers. But I fought for other blacks behind me. That was my duty. I took my stand. And I'm proud that I did. I can go to Lakeland now and sleep next door to white people or black people. That's the way it should be."

For 18 seasons in the majors, all with the same repainted batting helmet, Horton played with dignity and dug down when it mattered most. This included the most important throw in Detroit history to nail the Cardinals' Lou Brock at the plate in Game 5 of the '68 World Series.

Horton is understandably proud of his work with the Tigers—and of his late-career heroics with Seattle, when he was baseball's best designated hitter twice, as well as the league's Comeback Player of the Year at age 36. But he's much prouder of something else.

"It's all about getting involved in your community," he said. "There are a lot of Willie Hortons walking around. They're reaching out to the people the same way I did. I'd leave for the ballpark at noon and stop at a school, a playground or a hospital every day. We as black people have to do that. Our whole city does."

Horton was diagnosed with an aggressive form of prostate cancer in the spring of 2006. Suddenly, there was an outpouring of love—and a miracle.

"I'm a walking testimony that there's a loving God," Horton said. "I was getting ready for surgery when the doctor said, 'It's … not there.' When I think of all the letters I got this time, that's love. I walk through the park at age 64 and get turned on every day."

He can walk beyond the left-field fence and see his statue with the greatest of the great. Special assistants to the president like Horton can do that, remembering how far we've come—as far as any blast ever hit by Detroit's own "Willie the Wonder."

CHAPTER EIGHT

The Racial Healers

1968: FROM SOCIAL STRIFE TO GAME 7

FOR AT LEAST ONE TEAM, the '68 baseball season began on Sunday, October 1, 1967. When Dick McAuliffe hit into a double play for just the second time all year, the Tigers dropped Game 162 to California, 8-5. With its second doubleheader split in as many days, Detroit wound up one game back of Boston in a four-way scramble for the American League pennant.

After a summer scarred by a five-day riot and other unrest, a runner-up finish meant further frustration. For the Tigers to come so close and lose hurt more than a last-place finish ever could have. It also helped to produce the next world champions.

For six months and 10 days, Detroit was determined that '68 would be different. The Tigers made sure of that after a 7-3 loss to the Red Sox on Opening Day. Nine straight wins gave Mayo Smith's veterans the springboard they needed for a 103-59 finish, 12 games better than Baltimore.

We'll never know if the '68 team was the greatest in franchise history. You can make that pronouncement at your own peril if Kirk Gibson and Jack Morris are in earshot. Maybe it was. Maybe it wasn't. But it was as clear as the joy at Michigan and Trumbull that it was the most important team in Detroit sports history.

A six-month group hug helped heal a city. Instead of being blinded by hatred, fans across the state became color blind. A predominantly white team with three black stars proved beauty is only "win deep." And if a powder keg of problems didn't disappear, people of all ages and races bonded with pride and had a barrel of fun.

"It has almost become a cliché," Hall of Fame broadcaster Ernie Harwell said. "But like most clichés, it springs from a germ of truth. The '68 Tigers brought people together. Remember, the newspapers were on strike from November to mid-August. People needed something to listen to and root for. Whether they were green, black, or whatever, it got their minds off our sociological problems."

The only racial discord at the ballpark came when Harwell invited Jose Feliciano to sing a stylized rendition of "The Star-Spangled Banner" before Game 5 of the World Series. Otherwise, Detroit's first crowds of more than two million fans—2,031,847, to be exact—only saw blue and a little bit of orange.

And another song became an anthem of sorts. It was impossible to go anywhere in Michigan that summer and not hear a catchy tune with these lyrics:

> "We're all behind our baseball team.
> Go get 'em, Tigers!
> World Series-bound and pickin' up steam,
> Go get 'em, Tigers!
> There'll be joy in Tigertown,
> We'll sing this song,
> When the Bengals bring that pennant home
> Where it belongs.
> We're all behind our baseball team.
> Go get 'em, Deee-troit Tigers!
> Go get 'em, Tigers!"

The Tigers received nearly every honor available to man except the Nobel Peace Prize. Pitcher Denny McLain went 31-6, was an easy pick as the American League's Most Valuable Player and was a lock for the Cy Young Award. Catcher Bill

Freehan was second in the MVP balloting. And left fielder Willie Horton placed fourth on that list.

The most important thing was that the players realized their rightful place was atop the American League standings, a perch they hadn't occupied on the last day of the regular season since 1945. As Horton and right fielder Al Kaline remembered, that commitment began when the cheering stopped abruptly 12 months earlier.

"After the last game in '67, we stayed in the clubhouse for two or three hours," Horton said. "Then, we all got to spring training early. That's how close we were. With the papers on strike, all we had was radio. And I've never seen as many people hugging each other as I did that year."

"Losing on the last day the year before only made us more focused," Kaline said. "We went to spring training with a real passion and a goal to become world champions. We thought we had the best team and knew what it would take. A lot of us grew up together and trusted each other. I'm more proud of that than anything else in my career."

It was a strange team in many ways. Smith used 86 different batting orders, none for more than nine games. Detroit hit just .235—.001 below the major-league average in "The Year of the Pitcher." And slugging pitcher Earl Wilson had six more homers and hit .092 higher than regular shortstop Ray Oyler.

But it was a season filled with late-game heroics. If pinch-hitter extraordinaire Gates Brown didn't deliver in the clutch, some part-time player like backup infielder Tom Matchick did. It didn't matter that Matchick batted .203 that year. He delivered a ninth-inning homer that took the chirp out of the Orioles.

It was at about that time in mid-July that a baseball team became something much more. No amount of state aid or federal revenue sharing could have done what an ERA of 2.71 did. And no politician's words could have meant more than Detroit's 185 homers, plus another eight in the World Series—or 60 more than any other team.

"The Lord put us here to heal the city," Horton insisted. "I see that quote every day on the wall of the Tiger Club. We didn't have a lot of black players—me, Gates, Earl, John Wyatt, and, early in the year, Lenny Green. But I was proud to be a part of something bigger than ourselves."

Horton used to leave home at noon when the team was hosting a night game. He would always stop at a school, at a playground, or at Children's Hospital on his way to the stadium. A few hours later he would remember that the "D" on his left breast stood for Detroit, Determination, and Dignity.

In a season when Boston's Carl Yastrzemski led the league in hitting at .3005, Horton was fourth with a team-high .285 average. He also finished second with 36 homers, eight behind Washington slugger and soon-to-be-Tiger Frank Howard.

But Horton would be the first to tell you that Detroit's strength that year was its depth and its defense. It led the league in runs scored and fewest runs allowed, in slugging and on-base percentage, in baserunners allowed, and in fielding percentage.

McLain had a lot to do with that brilliance. At age 24, he had one of the greatest years any pitcher has experienced with an .838 winning percentage, 28 complete games, and a 1.96 ERA. He threw 336 innings, fanned 280, and surrendered just 241 hits. He also speared a liner from Baltimore's Boog Powell and started a triple play on September 1.

Wilson was only 13-12 but deserved better with a 2.85 ERA. Lefty Mickey Lolich was 17-9 with a 3.19 ERA. And former Ohio State quarterback Joe Sparma was the other starter in a four-man rotation.

"Nobody had a better one-two punch than McLain and Lolich," Kaline said. "We knew with either one of them on the mound, we had an excellent chance of winning. It made you feel good when you'd wake up in the morning and you knew McLain or Lolich was going to pitch. We knew they'd keep it close and we'd win it for them."

A bullpen by committee also made 27 starts. John Hiller threw a one-hitter against Chicago in the first game of a twinight doubleheader on August 20, just before McLain's fifth loss. And Pat Dobson, Daryl Patterson, Fred Lasher, Jon Warden, Wyatt, and Don McMahon each pitched in at least 20 games.

McAuliffe was the leadoff hitter again and a solid second baseman. He led the league with 95 runs, hit 16 homers, and paced the team with 10 triples and 82 walks. Making up for his last at-bat in '67, McAuliffe didn't hit into a double play in more than 650 opportunities. And he committed just nine errors, down from 28.

"We called him 'Mad Dog,'" Horton said of the former shortstop. "You should've seen him prepare! He didn't want anyone to talk to him before the game. But McAuliffe was a winner. He'd scrap and do whatever it took. He'd fight you if he had to."

McAuliffe did exactly that in the bottom of the third on August 22. After singling and scoring in the first for a 1-0 lead, he had just settled into an open stance that nearly every kid in Michigan imitated. Suddenly, Chicago southpaw Tommy John airmailed a pitch to the backstop. Ball four from a pitcher with great control was just as wild.

"I took about two steps to first and glared toward the mound," McAuliffe explained. "He said, 'What the hell are you looking at?' When I rushed at him, both benches emptied."

McAuliffe's knee made direct contact with John's left shoulder and ended his season. When No. 3 was suspended for five games and fined $250 by Joe Cronin, Campbell blasted the league president for "bad judgment." As with all the other adversity, it only made the Tigers stronger.

In a year when four American League teams hit 94 homers or less, Detroit had four players with 21 or more. Freehan had 25 homers and 84 RBIs, both career bests, and was hit by the pitch a league-high 24 times. First baseman Norm Cash had 25 homers in 127 games. And outfielder Jim Northrup had 21 dingers and was third in the American League with 90 RBIs.

The contributions didn't stop there. Third baseman Don Wert was selected as an All-Star, though he finished with only a

.200 average. Center fielder Mickey Stanley joined Freehan as a Gold Glove recipient. And Kaline hit .287 in just 102 games.

The two regular-season games no one in Detroit will ever forget were ninth-inning wins on Saturday, September 14, and the following Tuesday in Tiger Stadium.

A Horton single to left brought a 5-4 victory over Oakland and made McLain the first 30-game winner in 34 years. And no one did it in the next 38. It wasn't McLain's fault that 30-game winner Dizzy Dean was thrown out of the press box that day because he wasn't a member of the Baseball Writers Association of America.

Wert's single to right scored Kaline with the pennant-winning run on September 17, a 2-1 victory over the Yankees. Sparma held New York to five singles in nine innings and drove in the tying run with a single in the sixth. Three innings later, Wert finished the job after Kaline, Freehan, and Brown had reached base with two outs. Who cared that Baltimore had already been eliminated with a 2-0 loss to Boston?

"You start to wonder if you're ever going to play in a World Series," Kaline said. "You don't know if a team is going to trade you. And I wanted to stay here. I wanted to win a championship with Detroit."

Kaline missed a third of the '68 season with a broken arm. Before he returned he sat down with Smith and discussed a move that would have kept Horton, Stanley, and Northrup in the outfield—a forerunner of the switch that made Mayo famous.

"When I was coming off the disabled list, he wanted me to work out at third base," Kaline said. "That was the original idea. But when Willie got hurt, I went back to the outfield and really hit the ball well in September, when we won 11 in a row. Then, Mayo brought a couple of us into his office and said, 'I'm thinking of moving Mickey to shortstop.' We all said, 'Well, he is the best athlete we have.'"

"A lot of us had already talked about it," Horton said. "We wanted to get 'The Line' back in right. Ray Oyler was in on it, too. I think Northrup went to Stanley and said, 'You'll go to

After defeating the St. Louis Cardinals 4-1 in Game 7 of the World Series on October 10, 1968, Mickey Lolich jumps into the arms of catcher Bill Freehan as Dick McAuliffe joins in the celebration. *(Photo by Focus On Sport/Getty Images)*

short for the World Series. St. Louis only has one left-hander. Otherwise, you might not play.'"

No Tiger played in Game 1 against the Cardinals. Bob Gibson struck out 17 batters and out-dueled McLain in a 4-0 win at Busch Stadium. Lou Brock homered for St. Louis and continued his batting and base-running brilliance.

Lolich homered and beat Nelson Briles 8-1 in Game 2. Horton and Cash also left the yard to tie the series when it returned to Detroit. But Ray Washburn beat Wilson 7-3 in Game 3, thanks to homers by Tim McCarver and Orlando Cepeda. And Gibson fanned 10 more to beat McLain again, 10-4, in a rain-delayed Game 4. Brock led off with a homer, and Gibson added a shot to start the engraving on the MVP trophy.

But a funny thing happened on the way to another coronation for the defending champs. When Brock got greedy and tried to score from second on a sharp single in Game 5, Horton fired a strike to Freehan, who blocked the plate. Brock was retired, standing up. And with three runs in the seventh, Lolich had a 5-3 win and new life.

"I was a catcher all my life, and it took me a while to learn to throw from the outfield," Horton said. "But the key was knowing that, from the All-Star break on, Brock had a tendency to ease into bases. Preparation made that play possible."

Back in St. Louis for Game 6, Northrup and Kaline each hit his second home run of the week and McLain pitched Detroit to a 13-1 win. When Smith asked Lolich if he could go five innings, no one knew he would become the last pitcher to have three complete-game victories in a World Series.

When Gold Glove center fielder Curt Flood misplayed Northrup's blast in the top of the seventh, a bases-loaded triple off Gibson gave the Tigers a 3-0 lead. And when Freehan snared McCarver's foul pop-up for the 27th out, Detroit became the fourth of six teams to win Games 5, 6, and 7.

"If Flood hadn't slipped on that triple, they might still be playing," Harwell said.

Instead, a city and a state are still celebrating.

CHAPTER NINE

The Colorful Characters

CASH, McLAIN, FIDRYCH, AND GIBSON

NO SPORT LENDS ITSELF TO STATISTICS quite like major-league baseball. From RBI to ERA to OBP to WHIP, the numbers can often be numbing.

With Norm Cash, Denny McLain, Mark Fidrych, and Kirk Gibson, we remember their style as much as their stats. And they all had numbers we wouldn't have believed if we hadn't seen them in 1961, 1968, 1976, and 1984, respectively.

First baseman Norman Dalton Cash may be the most underrated Tiger in history. He is definitely one of the most colorful in a kaleidoscope of characters.

"I owe my success to expansion pitching, a short right-field fence, and my hollow bats," Cash joked with customary self-deprecation.

He could have credited a keen eye, his competitive spirit, and the ability to have fun in the face of adversity—from his American League debut with the Chicago White Sox in 1958 to his death in a boating accident off Beaver Island in 1986.

The 6-foot, 190-pound Texan began as a football star at Sul Ross State College, where he rushed for more than 1,500 yards as a junior in 1954. Cash was a 13th-round draft pick of the Chicago Bears but chose a different sport.

"Stormin' Norman" came to Detroit from Cleveland on April 12, 1960, in exchange for third baseman Steve Demeter, who would bat just five more times in the majors. But that deal was dwarfed when the Tigers acquired Rocky Colavito from the Indians for Harvey Kuenn five days later.

In their second season together, Colavito and Cash combined for 86 homers and 272 RBIs. Cash had 41 dingers, 132 RBIs, a .662 slugging average, and 124 walks. He led the league with 193 hits and a .487 on-base percentage—.039 higher than runner-up Mickey Mantle—and was a great return on a $13,000 salary.

But the big surprise in '61 was Cash's .361 batting average—.037 better than second-place Al Kaline. Though he hit 39 homers the following year, Cash's plunge to .243—a drop of .118—was the biggest for any batting champ.

No. 25 became the first Detroit player to hit a ball all the way out of Tiger Stadium, joining Ted Williams and Mantle in that exclusive club. Cash finished with four clouts over the right-field roof onto Trumbull Avenue, one more than Mantle.

A four-time All-Star, Cash showed his resilience by twice being named American League Comeback Player of the Year. He finished second in home runs three times and wound up behind only Kaline with 373 homers for Detroit and 212 dingers in Tiger Stadium.

Cash was an excellent fielder, especially on foul pops. He won two fielding titles and had two 50-game errorless streaks. Nine years after a World Series appearance with the White Sox, he led Detroit's starters with a .385 batting average in seven games against St. Louis.

But it was Cash's fun-loving spirit that won't be forgotten. Who else would've tried to call timeout when he was about to be tagged? Who else would've reported to the wrong base after a rain delay? And who else would've brought a piano leg to the plate for the last out of Nolan Ryan's second no-hitter?

Off the field, Cash loved the nightlife and could smell a party a mile away. The best party in town was usually wherever he was.

Cash was always a corker, even without a bat in his hands, and should be on the Wall of Fame at Comerica Park.

"I used to call Norm 'The John Wayne of Baseball,'" 12-year teammate Willie Horton said. "He'd say, 'Give me a Marlboro and a Budweiser, and I'll be out there.' I'd look at him and say, 'How's he ever going to play today?' He'd sit in the whirlpool, then go out and help you win. Norm lived a hard life. But you put him between those lines, and you'd go to war with a guy like him."

Cash was one of the last players never to wear a batting helmet. And when reminded he'd struck out 1,091 times, he said, "Do you realize at 500 at-bats a year, that means I played more than two years and never touched the ball?" Instead, Cash touched people everywhere he went.

"Every time I think of Norm, I get a smile on my face," Kaline said. "He never got all the credit he deserved. He was a great teammate. I miss him every day."

Dennis Dale McLain missed what should've been the second half of a Hall of Fame career. Instead, a player claimed on waivers from the White Sox in 1963 became a member of the Hall of Shame with two suspensions from baseball and two stints in federal prison.

"He's the original flim-flam man," 1968 World Series hero Jim Northrup said in ESPN Classic's *SportsCentury* series. "Any day I expect him to come riding in on a Conestoga wagon, selling elixir out of the back end as he's leaving town—probably being run out of town. But that's Denny!"

McLain and Northrup once got into it during a card game at the team hotel and had to be separated. But No. 17 separated himself with a 31-6 mark on the mound in '68, the year he was the American League MVP and won the first of two straight Cy Young Awards.

Even in a year with ridiculous pitching numbers, McLain's 1.96 ERA, his 280 strikeouts, and the only 30-win season in the last 72 years speak volumes. Drinking a case of Pepsi a day, he was almost as good the next year with a 24-9 mark, a 2.80 ERA, and nine shutouts.

That ERA could've been better if McLain hadn't cooked up a plan with catcher Jim Price to feed Mantle a fat batting-practice pitch for his final homer in Tiger Stadium.

But when No. 17 was right, there was nobody better. As announcer and occasional songwriter Ernie Harwell wrote: "Denny McLain, Denny McLain. . . . There's never been any like Denny McLain."

If his pitch on the organ was perfect, and it was close enough to earn a recording deal and gigs in Las Vegas, McLain didn't always make beautiful music with teammates. That was particularly true with fellow pitching star Mickey Lolich, who accepted a ride in McLain's plane to the 1969 All-Star Game, only to be stranded there without warning.

McLain's world began to collapse in 1970 when *Sports Illustrated* documented his role in a bookmaking operation in 1967. It was alleged that his toes were dislocated by a stomp from mobster Tony Giacalone over a $46,000 payout.

In February 1970, Commissioner Bowie Kuhn responded to the evidence and suspended McLain until July 1. Once reinstated, McLain went 3-5, dumped ice water on reporters Jim Hawkins and Watson Spoelstra, and was suspended again after waving a gun in a Chicago restaurant. In the off-season McLain was dealt to Washington, where he went 10-22 in 1971 and feuded with my-way-or-the-highway manager Ted Williams.

"The problem with Denny was that he always pushed the envelope," Harwell said. "He went over the edge. He had a lot of personality, a lot of charm, and a lot of intelligence. But where Norm was able to stop before he hurt the team, Denny was more his own guy. As for the injury in '67, I'm not sure anybody knows the true story. Denny's story was that he was asleep on the couch, got up in a hurry, and hurt his foot."

At various times he also suggested he kicked his locker after a bad performance, then said he kicked garbage cans after being terrorized by squirrels.

McLain hurt himself again, along with those who trusted him, when the cheering stopped in 1972 after just 10 major-league seasons. Ballooning from 185 pounds to more than 300, he was found guilty on racketeering, extortion, and narcotics charges in 1985. McLain was sentenced to 23 years in prison but had that conviction overturned for procedural violations.

After a stint in talk radio, he bought a meat processing company that went bankrupt. McLain and an associate were suspected of stealing $12.5 million from the pension fund and later sentenced to eight years for conspiracy, theft, money laundering, and mail fraud. He served more than six years, professing his innocence on all charges.

No one was more innocent than Mark Steven Fidrych, who hit the big time in 1976 but never stopped pinching himself. Fidrych's good fortune was almost as good for some frustrated fans, who had just endured a 57-win season.

Like McLain, "The Bird" was on the cover of *Sports Illustrated* at the peak of his popularity. The difference? McLain was in big trouble. Fidrych posed with Big Bird of *Sesame Street*.

A 10th-round selection in the 1974 amateur draft, the pride of Northborough, Massachusetts, burst onto the scene two years later like the brightest fireworks for America's Bicentennial.

Fidrych had a no-hitter for seven innings and settled for a two-hit, 2-1 win in his first major-league start. And when he beat the Yankees 5-1 in less than two hours on ABC's *Monday Night Baseball*, the love-in was on.

Less than three months later, he was the American League starter and losing pitcher in the All-Star Game. No. 20 wound up 19-9 with a 2.34 ERA and 24 complete games.

But the Fidrych phenomenon was more than the stats that made him Rookie of the Year and the runner-up to Jim Palmer for the Cy Young Award. It was all about having fun and doing things no other ballplayer had done.

Who else would crouch down and manicure the mound each inning? Who else would talk to the ball or himself or anyone

Mark Fidrych, one of the Tigers' most colorful players, pitches during a game at Tiger Stadium in Detroit, Michigan. *(Photo by Tony Tomsic/MLB Photos via Getty Images)*

who'd listen? And who else would throw balls back to the umpire with bizarre requests?

"That ball has a hit in it," Fidrych said. "I want it to get back in the ball bag and goof around with the other balls in there. Maybe it'll learn some sense and come out as a pop-up next time."

At 6-foot-3, he drove a subcompact car and lived in a small apartment. He wore jeans at every opportunity. And he couldn't have paid for the postage to answer half his fan mail on a salary of $16,500 a year.

The Tigers made much more than that in each of his 18 home appearances in '76, when nearly half the season's attendance showed up and the nation fell in love from afar. Economists estimated a $1-million boon from "The Bird." And after the season Detroit gave him a $25,000 bonus, then signed him to a three-year deal for $255,000.

He returned the money his adoring followers sent and didn't hire an agent or take full advantage of his opportunities that year.

"Sometimes I get lazy and let the dishes stack up," Fidrych said. "But they don't stack too high. I only have four dishes."

He had the love of a state and much of a nation. But he also had bad luck with injuries and started just 27 more games his final four seasons, going 10-10 for teams that never finished higher than fourth. A torn rotator cuff that never healed ended his joyride.

"Fidrych was an overnight celebrity and a product of television," Harwell said. "He barely made the team coming north. But Mark brought back the curtain call. The people wouldn't let him leave. He was the most charismatic Tiger ever. I've heard baseball people say if he hadn't gotten hurt, he wouldn't have been that good the next year. And I've heard others say he was the kind of guy who could've pitched for years. He hurt his knee shagging flies in the outfield, then compensated and hurt his arm."

Kirk Harold Gibson hurt opposing pitchers and hammered some seats in the upper deck in right field in Tiger Stadium, most notably with a three-run shot off Rich "Goose" Gossage in the eighth inning of Game 5 to seal the '84 World Series.

Much like the Cardinals' Bob Gibson 20 years earlier, he loved the spotlight. And he wrote a book with Lynn Henning, *Bottom of the Ninth*, just after he hobbled to the plate in that situation and one-armed a backdoor slider into the seats at Dodger Stadium to decapitate the Oakland A's in the '88 Series.

Having seen Gibson play football and traumatize teams for four seasons under Darryl Rogers at Michigan State, it was clear why many believed he'd have been one of the best receivers in NFL history. At 6-foot-3, 227 pounds on MSU's Pro Day in 1978, the slowest clocking any scout had for his 40-yard dash was 4.28 seconds. Plus, he loved to hit linebackers every bit as much as baseballs.

He loved to hit the party scene, too. With sidekick and eventual brother-in-law Dave Rozema, the pranks and horseplay ranked with any revelry in franchise history—even Cash's nights on the town with the human Mardi Gras, manager Billy Martin.

"Being from Michigan—me from Grand Rapids and Kirk from Waterford—and playing with the Tigers, it was wild," Rozema said. "Being single and making money we never thought we'd have, it was a dream come true. You had to be bad!"

Billed as "The Next Mantle" by another manager, Sparky Anderson, Gibson had to work on being a man first. He was completely capable of belting a 523-foot home run or going into a 9-for-73 slump. But he fought everything and everyone, including himself. It wasn't until he got help at the Pacific Institute in 1983, the worst year of his life, that he began to harness his vast potential.

"Gibby" was never warm and fuzzy, despite a boiling temper and all types of facial hair. He was cold. He was Kirk. And he was one of the fiercest competitors any sport has seen—think Scott Skiles' mind in Bo Jackson's body.

"Gibson brought something to the game that a lot of people loved," Harwell said. "He wasn't polished and wasn't schooled. He burst onto the scene and learned on the job. But he always had great passion and pride. He was a great team guy and a great clutch guy. Most people get nervous at a time like that. Others rise to the occasion."

MSU coach Danny Litwhiler saw that before Gibson did and wouldn't let him quit after an 0-for-12 start in his only year of college baseball. Eventually, Gibson rose like a majestic homer and learned some things along the way. His education continues.

CHAPTER TEN

The Wire-to-Wire Winners

1984: FROM 35-5 TO GAME 5

IT WAS THE BEST START ANY BASEBALL TEAM HAS HAD. And it began almost six months before Opening Day.

After the Detroit Tigers won 92 games and finished six games behind the world champion Orioles in 1983, important events in October, December, and March turned a good team into one of the greatest in history just one year later.

On October 11, 1983, Tigers owner John Fetzer shocked almost everyone and sold the team to Domino's Pizza founder Tom Monaghan for roughly $54 million. Monaghan never got a hit or retired a batter. But at least initially, his purchase was a long home run. The '84 attendance—2,704,794—was 672,947 more than had ever been seen at the corner of Michigan and Trumbull.

In early December, outfielder Kirk Gibson was low as he had ever been—and not just because he hit .227 in '83. Just the thought of going to work made him sick. And it didn't matter that his manager and many of his teammates thought he was an idiot. Gibson finally agreed with them.

Atop his horse, Rusty, and with his golden retriever, Nick, alongside, Gibson rode through the woods for two hours and finally stopped at the top of a hill, staring into the wind and snow. There, he had an epiphany and realized his life had to change.

Following a world championship season, Kirk Gibson looks on from the dugout during spring training in March of 1985. *(Photo by Andrew D. Bernstein/Getty Images)*

It turned 180 degrees when his agent quickly arranged a meeting in Seattle with Frank Bartenetti of the Pacific Institute, a clinic for the mind and soul. When Gibson discarded his negative thoughts and began a process of visualization, it was easy to see he was a new man. Pitchers learned that the hard way when Gibson hit .287 and increased his homers from 15 to 27, his RBIs from 51 to 91, and his steals from 14 to 29.

But Detroit needed more pitching, too. On March 27, 1984, Sparky Anderson's team got that—and more—when it acquired reliever Willie Hernandez and first baseman Dave Bergman from Philadelphia for outfielder Glenn Wilson and catcher John Wockenfuss.

In 74 games the previous year with the Cubs and Phillies, Hernandez was solid but seldom spectacular as a southpaw set-up man. With nine wins, eight saves, and a 3.28 ERA, no one knew how much his addition would mean.

It started when the Tigers went 9-0, 16-1, 19-2, 26-4, and, finally, 35-5—the winningest first quarter of a season any team has had. That dominance continued in a 104-58 regular season, 15 games better than runner-up Toronto, in a three-game sweep of Kansas City for the American League pennant and a 4-1 romp over San Diego in the World Series.

The toughest challenge Detroit could have had was to face the 1968 Tigers in a fantasy matchup—more on that later.

From Jack Morris' no-hitter against Chicago in the fourth game of the year to Gibson's three-run, Series-clinching blast in the next-to-last inning against the Padres, Detroit wasn't just good. It was dominant.

The Tigers joined the 1927 Yankees and the '55 Dodgers as the only teams to lead wire-to-wire and win it all. Detroit's 111 wins, counting postseason play, were four more than any total in franchise history.

WDIV sports anchor Al Ackerman coined the phase "Bless You Boys!" early in the year. A song with that message soon followed. And even some agnostics agreed. The '84 Bengals were blessed, indeed.

"We didn't think we were ever going to lose," pitcher Dave Rozema said. "We knew we couldn't play 35-5 ball forever. But the breaks all went our way. I just thank God we started that fast. Toronto had a great, young ballclub."

The Tigers had a better group of maturing stars and tremendous balance. They led the American League with 829 runs, 187 homers, and a .342 on-base percentage on offense, along with 11.9 runners per game and a 3.49 ERA on defense.

Individually, they were led at the plate by catcher Lance Parrish's 33 homers and 98 RBIs and shortstop Alan Trammell's 174 hits and .314 batting average. The pitching was paced by Morris, 19-11 with a 3.60 ERA, and underrated Dan Petry, 18-8 with a .3.24 ERA. But none of that would have mattered without Hernandez's 1.92 ERA and 32 saves, not counting three in the postseason.

Much of the credit for Hernandez's emergence belonged to pitching coach Roger Craig. But it almost seemed that American League hitters had never seen a screwball before they got a look at Hernandez—whether you called him Willie or Guillermo.

If strength up the middle is crucial for champions, Detroit had everything it needed to claim its first title in 16 years. Aside from the league's best pitching, Parrish, Trammell, and second baseman Lou Whitaker all won Gold Gloves for fielding excellence. And center fielder Chet Lemon was one of the best in the business.

The rest of the lineup wasn't bad, either. Left fielder Larry Herndon was a solid every day contributor. And, at age 37, designated hitter-first baseman Darrell Evans was fine on the field and better in the clubhouse.

Anderson was named American League Manager of the Year for the first time and often was asked how his latest team compared to the "Big Red Machine" he led to two crowns in Cincinnati. It was a lot like asking a parent which child he or she preferred. Anderson was way too smart to choose.

Despite Morris' gem, the best moment of the regular season had to be first baseman Dave Bergman's 10th-inning homer against Toronto after fouling off 13 pitches. Some innings take less time than Bergman's best at-bat.

"I just swung and closed my eyes," Bergman said of a classic confrontation with winter-ball teammate Leroy Jackson.

Morris, Petry, and Milt Wilcox took care of business in the playoffs, as the Royals managed just four runs and 18 hits in 27 innings. Herndon, Trammell, and Parrish homered to support Morris in an 8-1 win in Game 1. Gibson helped Petry, Hernandez, and Aurelio Lopez win in Game 2 in Kansas City. And Wilcox and Hernandez combined for a three-hit shutout in Game 3 in Tiger Stadium.

That set up a showdown with San Diego, a Cinderella representative from the National League. The Padres were 92-70 in the regular season, then rallied from a 2-0 deficit to beat Chicago in five games, thanks to the bat of first baseman Steve Garvey and some of the Cubs' gloves.

Starting on the road in a 2-3-2 travel format, Detroit knew a split of the first two games in Jack Murphy Stadium would mean it could sweep the next three at home and not have to return to San Diego unless it wanted to visit Southern California for a winter vacation.

That's exactly what happened, establishing the '84 Tigers as one of the top teams ever to play the game. They met every challenge with pride and passion. They just couldn't beat teams in the postseason that didn't get there.

Game 1 of the World Series was a 3-2 Detroit triumph. Herndon homered again. Morris beat Mark Thurmond, scattering eight hits in a complete-game effort. And the home-field advantage shifted.

The Padres showed a pulse in Game 2, handing the Tigers a 3-0 first-inning lead and rallying for a 5-3 win. Petry was tagged with the loss, yielding a homer to Kurt Bevacqua before giving way to Lopez, Fred Scherrer, Doug Bair, and Hernandez.

Game 3 was a 5-2 Detroit victory, thanks to 11 walks. Third baseman Marty Castillo hit a two-run homer. Wilcox got the win with help from Scherrer and Hernandez.

The Saturday game was Trammell's day, and Morris was the beneficiary in a 4-2 triumph. With Whitaker on base in the bottom of the first, Trammell greeted Eric Show with a two-run shot. And in the same situation two innings later, the Series MVP made it 4-1 with a distant replay.

That set the stage for the Tigers' fourth and last championship, an 8-4 win on October 14 that is still emblazoned in our memories. A crowd of 51,901 was announced, though 10 times that many have said they were there.

The revelry lasted well into the night and included the burning of a police car. That photo, distributed worldwide, did more to hurt Detroit's image than any single event, with the possible exception of the '67 riots. It also stole the spotlight from a team that deserved it with one last W.

The Tigers exploded for three runs in the bottom of the first, including a two-run blast by Gibson. But when Petry was touched for three runs in less than four innings, Anderson wasted no time in going to his bullpen. Scherrer, Lopez, and Hernandez took it from there and allowed one meaningless run the rest of the way.

Gibson put Detroit ahead in the fifth, scoring from third on a pop-up that second baseman Alan Wiggins caught backpedaling on the outfield grass. Parrish homered in the seventh to make it 5-3 before the Padres got one run back in the eighth.

Trailing 5-4, San Diego thought All-Star closer Rich "Goose" Gossage would keep it close and give the visitors one more shot. Apparently, no one asked Gibson.

With runners on second and third and one out, No. 23 headed to the plate with all the confidence of a former Chicago Bull with the same number. From that point on, the Padres didn't have a prayer.

Manager Dick Williams wanted Gossage to load the bases and set up a double play. But after owning Gibson for years in the American League, Gossage was sure he could get another strikeout. There was no Tiger he'd have preferred to face. And did he ever get his wish!

Anderson held four fingers in the air, figuring the intentional walk was imminent. But Gibson knew how Gossage's mind worked. His own mind worked much the same way.

Turning toward Anderson in the third-base dugout, Gibson offered a $10 bet that Gossage would pitch to him—and that the ball would become a treasured souvenir.

The nation could read Anderson's lips when he repeated in his best Sparky-ese, "He don't want to walk you!" A master psychologist, he knew exactly which buttons to push. But that wasn't necessary—not this time and not with this team. History was waiting to be written. Gibson stood ready—a pen in one hand, a bat in the other.

"I really thought they were going to walk him," broadcaster Ernie Harwell said of what would become one of history's most famous calls. "Knowing they had first base open, I was sure they would. But I don't know if Gibson had ever had a hit off Gossage. I know he struck out a lot."

Maybe a different Gibson did. But remember the visualization training? Gibson remembered it well and said to himself, "It's out of here!"

Gossage's first fastball—what else?—was wide. Ball one.

The second delivery was another screamer. It screamed in at close to 100 mph. It screamed out to the upper deck in right field. And it left nearly everyone screaming, especially Gibson, as he loped around the bases and gave a famous double-crank arm thrust.

The other key figures in an essential off-season both had their moments, too. Hernandez shut the door in the ninth, with the final out a fly to Herndon. And with the media filing stories or unable to leave with the disturbance outside, Monaghan had pizzas helicoptered to second base.

That only leaves one question. Who could beat the '84 Tigers?

Detroit's '68 team would've loved that chance, as this exchange between Rozema and Gates Brown at a pregame autograph session last summer showed:

Rozema: "It might've been like it was when they beat St. Louis in '68. Mickey Lolich would've been tough on our left-handers. Denny McLain? I don't know about him. But maybe our speed would've gotten to them. They were a slower ballclub."

Brown: "I could run!"

Rozema: "Gator could run. But he was on the bench! He had to get on first."

Brown: "You say it'd be like it was with St. Louis. What makes you think it'd even go seven?"

Rozema: "It would!"

Brown: "Arrrgh! … We'd have knocked you off in about five—no more than six!"

Rozema: "It might've come down to 'Ol' Rosie' then! The '68 Tigers could hit the fastball."

Brown: "We could hit the stuff you threw, too. You'd have kept doing this (whipping his head around to find the ball as it left the park)."

Rozema: "Why do you think the fans loved me so much? They'd say, 'Rosie's pitching today!' And the left-field stands were always full."

Both agreed on one thing. They would have liked their chances against the 2006 team. And with the '84 Tigers, could you imagine Trammell facing Kenny Rogers or Gibson trying to go deep off Joel Zumaya?

Where can we get a couple of tickets?

CHAPTER ELEVEN

The Other Roars

1907-1909, '34-35, '40, '45, '61, '67, '72, '87

THE 1968 AND 1984 DETROIT TIGERS get all the love—and appropriately so. They should be revered, here and elsewhere.

The 2006 heroes are fresh in our minds and forever safe in our memories. The thrills and chills still shoot down our spines.

But 11 other teams in franchise history are worthy of belated hugs. They represent five generations of devoted Detroit baseball fans.

Let's start at the beginning with the city's only three-peat pennant-winners and the first players in either league to do that, Hughie Jennings' clubs from 1907-1909.

Led by the brilliance of human hit machine Ty Cobb, the 1907 Tigers improved from sixth to first and from 71 wins to 92 in Jennings' first season, edging the Athletics by a game and a half in the American League.

Few players have ever been as important to their team and their sport as Cobb was at age 20. He led the American League with 212 hits, 119 RBIs, and a .350 batting average for his first titles in those departments—21 more hits, 27 more RBIs, and .027 higher than anyone else. Cobb was also No. 1 with 283 total bases, a .468 slugging percentage, and 53 steals.

He had help from outfield mates Sam Crawford and Davy Jones, who reached base often enough to finish one-two in runs scored with 102 and 101, respectively. Cobb was third with 97.

It was the way he played, not just the numbers he posted, that made Cobb such an incredible force. The running game was here to stay. And so was "The Georgia Peach" for the next two decades.

"Wild Bill" Donovan and Ed Killian each won 25 games for Jennings in 1907. Donovan had only four losses, Killian a 1.78 ERA.

None of that mattered in Detroit's first World Series. After a 12-inning tie, the Tigers dropped four in a row to the Chicago Cubs by a combined score of 16-3. They never scored more than one run or lost by less than two.

Detroit won 90 games in 1908 and beat Cleveland by a half-game. Donovan shut out the White Sox on the last day of the season, and the Tigers weren't forced to make up a rainout. That glaring inequity led to a rule change.

In a season when American League hitters averaged just .239, their lowest figure until 1967, Cobb won his second batting title with a .324 mark. In an "off year" by his standards, he also led in hits, doubles, triples, RBIs, and slugging percentage.

Crawford was No. 1 in the league in homers with seven. And he finished between Matty McIntyre and Germany Schaefer in another top-three sweep of the runs category.

Despite scoring 78 more times than any opponent in the regular season, Detroit lost to the Cubs in October again. The Tigers won 8-3 in Game 3 but were outscored 21-7 in the other four contests, including a pair of shutouts to end it.

Cobb's last chance for a championship was a 98-win season in 1909. Capturing the Triple Crown with nine homers, 107 RBIs, and a .377 average, he also topped the Junior Circuit with 116 runs, 216 hits, 296 total bases, and 76 steals.

George Mullin led both leagues with 29 victories and a .784 winning percentage.

But after losing the odd-numbered games and winning the even ones, Detroit was blanked in the final game of the World Series for the third time in a row. This time, Pittsburgh did the honors, as Cobb batted just .231.

It was there that Cobb's legend grew. After reaching base for the first time in the Series, he reportedly hollered down to Pirates shortstop and batting champ Honus Wagner, "I'm comin' down on the next pitch, krauthead!" When Cobb did exactly that, Wagner applied the tag with authority and growled, "Get back in your cage, animal."

The 1934 Tigers struggled early, started to climb in June and July, and streaked past the Yankees with a 23-6 August. Their 101-53 record was seven games better than New York's and the winningest mark in Detroit until 1968.

Manager-catcher Mickey Cochrane, acquired from Philadelphia, was the American League MVP, though his numbers couldn't match the contributions of second baseman Charlie Gehringer, first baseman Hank Greenberg, or pitchers Lynwood "Schoolboy" Rowe and Tommy Bridges.

Gehringer led the league with 134 runs and 214 hits, finishing second to Yankees first baseman Lou Gehrig with a .356 average. Greenberg led both leagues with 63 doubles. And Bridges had a 16-game winning streak.

But it was Rowe who led the staff with 24 triumphs and became the talk of the nation after a guest appearance on Eddie Cantor's radio show. When Rowe punctuated an answer by whispering, "How am I doin', Edna, honey?" to his sweetheart, Edna Mary Skinner, Cantor had a new catchphrase and opponents had a ready-made taunt.

Detroit liked its chances in the '34 World Series but fell to St. Louis in seven games. The Tigers led 3-2, then dropped the last two at home, including an 11-0 debacle in Game 7. When Cardinals star Joe "Ducky" Medwick took out third baseman Marv Owen on a tag play, he was pelted with so much debris he was ordered to leave Briggs Stadium for his own safety by Commissioner Kenesaw Mountain Landis.

Hank Greenberg, first baseman for the Detroit Tigers, hits a home run on Opening Day against the Chicago White Sox on April 20, 1938.
(Photo by Mark Rucker/Transcendental Graphics, Getty Images)

With 93 wins in 1935, Detroit beat New York again, this time by three games. A hot July gave the Tigers a lead. And they survived a late slump to win back-to-back pennants in Greenberg's first of two MVP seasons.

"Hammerin' Hank" had 121 runs, 203 hits, 46 doubles, 36 homers, and 170 RBIs—51 more than runner-up Lou Gehrig. Meanwhile, Bridges and Rowe combined for 40 wins and were one-two in strikeouts.

Facing the Cubs again in October, Detroit dropped the opener 3-0 at home and suffered a tough blow in Game 2. After homering to give his team a quick lead, Greenberg broke his wrist in a collision with catcher Gabby Hartnett a few innings later and was reduced to a cheerleader's role.

The Tigers went on to win that day, 8-3. With 6-5 and 2-1 wins in Chicago, Detroit was one triumph from its first World Championship. And after Chicago stayed alive, 3-1, Cochrane's team finished the job with a 4-3 victory in Game 6.

Goose Goslin's ninth-inning single scored Cochrane, gave Bridges his second win of the Series and made a hero of unheralded outfielder Pete Fox, who had 10 hits and batted .385. Gehringer had nine hits and batted .375.

With the Red Wings claiming the Stanley Cup, the Lions winning the NFL title, and hometown hero Joe Louis about to rule boxing's heavyweight division, the Tigers' ascension to the top made Detroit "The City of Champions."

Five years later under Del Baker's direction, the Tigers went from fifth to first and won 90 games, one more than Cleveland, which lost its lead after a player rebellion against manager Ossie Vitt. In the clincher, Floyd Giebell blanked the Indians and beat the great Bob Feller for his third and final major-league victory.

Detroit's magic disappeared in a terrific 1940 World Series. The Cincinnati Reds, who won 100 games in the regular season, took four more despite Greenberg's heroics—10 hits, four for extra bases, and a .357 average.

The best story was the heart of Tigers pitcher Bobo Newsom, who beat the Reds 7-2 in Game 1 and 8-0 in Game 5. His father died in the middle of the Series. But Newsom took the ball for Game 7 on two days' rest and lost 2-1 in a pitching duel with Paul Derringer.

After finishing one game behind the St. Louis Browns in 1944, Detroit won just 88 times the following season but still finished a game and a half ahead of runner-up Washington in the last year of World War II.

Returning to the U.S. from Asia at mid-season, Greenberg's ninth-inning grand slam beat the Browns on the season's last day and clinched Detroit's fourth World Series appearance in 12 years.

That couldn't have happened without Hal Newhouser's brilliance in a second-straight MVP season. He pitched more than 313 innings, won 25 games, and had a 1.81 ERA for Steve O'Neill's club.

After being bombed 9-0 by the Cubs in the Series opener, Newhouser watched Virgil Trucks and Dizzy Trout win 4-1 decisions in the second and fourth games, respectively. "Prince Hal" took it from there, winning Game 5 8-4 and Game 7 9-3 at Wrigley Field.

The Tigers weren't as fortunate 16 years later. With 101 wins, eight more than the National League champion Reds, Detroit still wound up eight games behind one of the best teams in baseball history, the power-laden '61 Yankees.

Bob Scheffing's team was only a game and a half out in August when it went to New York for a three-game weekend set. But the Tigers lost every game by one run, starting with Whitey Ford's shutout in the opener. Case closed.

That doesn't change some tremendous numbers. First baseman Norm Cash had one of the greatest seasons in the last half-century, coming out of nowhere to bat a league-best .361 with 41 homers and 132 RBIs. And Cash wasn't the primary power source. Left-fielder Rocky Colavito hit 45 homers and drove home 140 runs.

"We scored an awful lot of runs that year," runner-up for the batting crown Al Kaline said. "We just couldn't get past the

Yankees. To win 100 games and not make the postseason is almost unheard of these days. Usually, you win the pennant."

Kaline and Cash chased a championship till the final day of the season in 1967. But a pair of doubleheader splits with the Angels on the season's final weekend left Detroit tied for second with Minnesota, one game behind the Red Sox and baseball's last Triple Crown winner, Carl Yastrzemski.

In their first year under Mayo Smith, the Tigers got 22 wins from Earl Wilson and a fine all-around season from catcher Bill Freehan, who finished third in the MVP voting.

Amid the fires of a burning city, that near-miss lit the flame for Detroit's '68 heroes. And if it took two years to produce one title, that sure beats a 23-year drought.

"The best thing about '67 was that it set the tone for '68," left-fielder and home-grown hero Willie Horton said. "We knew we had the best team in the league in '67. But I had my Achilles operated on, and Al missed about a month. We had to believe, between the two of us, we'd have made at least one game's difference!"

The difference in 1972 was that many of the same players finished one win ahead of Boston, not one behind them. When the players went on strike in spring training, the first 13 days of the season were cancelled. Thus, Detroit wound up playing 156 games, the Red Sox just 155.

At 86-50, thanks in large part to Mickey Lolich's 22 wins, the rapidly aging Tigers were good enough to win the American League East Division. But against an emerging Oakland powerhouse that won 93 games, Billy Martin's men came up short in a best-of-five series with precious little scoring.

Detroit should have realized it wouldn't be easy after the regular season. Northrup led the starters in hitting at just .261— a full 100 points below Cash's average 11 years earlier. And when "Stormin' Norman" led the way with 22 homers and 61 RBIs, those totals were less than half of the team highs in 1961.

Regardless, the Tigers gave "The Swingin' A's" all they wanted. It just didn't seem that way when the teams met in Oakland.

Lolich pitched into the 11th but was tagged with a 3-2 loss in Game 1, despite solo homers from Cash and Kaline. In Game 2, Detroit's hitting was handcuffed in a three-hit shutout by John "Blue Moon" Odom.

Back in Tiger Stadium for the rest of the week, Detroit got a homer from Freehan and a seven-hit shutout from Joe Coleman in Game 3. And though Lolich pitched into the 10th in Game 4, it took a three-run rally in the bottom of that inning for Detroit to win 4-3, with closer John Hiller the pitcher of record.

That took the teams to Game 5 and an Odom-Fryman match-up. After the Tigers got a run in the bottom of the first, Odom and Vida Blue slammed the door the rest of the way. When the A's drew even in the top of the second and took a 2-1 lead in the top of the fourth, that was all the offense they needed to reach the World Series. There, they beat a Cincinnati team directed by Sparky Anderson.

It took a dozen years before Detroit saw postseason play again in 1984. And most of those world champions were there three years later when Anderson's Tigers won 98 games, edged Toronto in the American League East and met Minnesota in the best-of-seven playoffs.

The Twins, an 85-win team, were a decided underdog. But they took a two-game lead when they dealt recently acquired Doyle Alexander an 8-5 setback and beat Jack Morris 6-4 in the Metrodome.

Detroit avoided a sweep when Walt Terrell and Mike Henneman outlasted Oakland 7-6 in Game 3. But Minnesota finished the job in Tiger Stadium. Frank Viola out-pitched Frank Tanana 5-3 in Game 4. And Bert Blyleven and the bullpen beat Alexander and three relievers, 9-5.

"That Twins team that won was a real shock," *ESPN Baseball Encyclopedia* editor Gary Gillette said. "Alan Trammell had an MVP kind of year. And this was still a Whitaker-Gibson-Morris team—one that really should've gone to the World Series."

Detroit also dealt pitching prospect John Smoltz to Atlanta for the 37-year-old Alexander, a great deal in the stretch run, but a costly giveaway since 1989.

CHAPTER TWELVE

The Men In Charge

HUGHIE, MICKEY, MAYO, BILLY, AND SPARKY

THE BEST MANAGERS HAVE ONE THING IN COMMON. They win a lot more than they lose. Nothing else matters in the won-or-done world of major league baseball.

Hughie Jennings, Mickey Cochrane, Mayo Smith, Billy Martin, and Sparky Anderson all understood that fact before directing the Detroit Tigers in postseason play. So did Jim Leyland, who led Florida to a stunning world championship in 1997 and finished 52 games out of first place the following year.

It didn't hurt that Jennings had Ty Cobb terrorizing opponents with his flaming bat and flashing spikes, or that Cochrane had Charlie Gehringer and Hank Greenberg, a one-two punch in Detroit second only to Joe Louis' fists.

And it didn't hurt that Smith had baseball's last 31-game winner, Denny McLain, in 1968, that Martin had veterans who could—and did—fill out their own lineup card, or that Anderson was handed closer Willie Hernandez, the American League MVP in 1984, in a trade a week before the season started.

That's about the way it works. Make a great trade and the manager looks like a Mensa member. Make a mess of the team, and the next trade might involve the manager himself, as it did when the Tigers shipped Jimmy Dykes to Cleveland for Joe Gordon in a unique strife-swap in 1960.

But let's take a look—and if you close your eyes, a listen—to Detroit's dictators of the dugout, beginning with the great entertainer, Hugh Ambrose Jennings, baseball's "Eee-Yah" man.

A standout shortstop in the 1890s, Jennings was hit by pitches a record 287 times. If that had been Cobb, there may have been a couple of homicides. But Jennings settled disputes differently, as seen by his enrollment in Cornell's law school in 1899.

Managing the Tigers for 14 seasons from 1907-1920, Jennings debuted with three straight pennants but lost twice to the Cubs and once to the Pirates in the World Series. A greater feat may have been his ability to get along with the often-antisocial Cobb, who took over as the team's player-manager in 1921.

Without question, the jovial Irishman and "The Georgia Peach" had time to bond. For nearly a decade and a half, Jennings would man the first-base coaching box. And Cobb would often stop at first on his way to second.

Jennings' trademark in Detroit was a one-legged dance with his arms raised high and the rallying cry, "Heeere we are!" Over time, through painless contractions and the loss of consonants, that chant became "Eee-Yah!" and rang through Bennett Park and Navin Field.

When Jennings passed his bar exam while managing the Tigers, he paved the way for would-be lawyer Tony La Russa to live his dream without apologies. Appropriately, when Jennings lost a battle with the bottle and bowed out, his mark was 1,184-995—.543. After 28 years with the White Sox, Athletics, and Cardinals, La Russa sits at .536.

And to think that Jennings' managerial career nearly ended before it began. While in law school, he suffered two skull fractures after a springboard dive into an empty pool.

Gordon Stanley Cochrane was every bit as tough and just as fearless. Best known as a Hall of Fame catcher with the Philadelphia Athletics from 1925-33, "Black Mike" was shipped to Detroit for catcher Johnny Pasek and cash. He promptly became a terrific player-manager and earned his second MVP award in 1934.

Cochrane's numbers that year were good, not great: 74 runs, 140 hits, two home runs, 76 RBIs, and a .320 batting average—30 runs and 13 homers below his last totals under Connie Mack. But his leadership meant everything to a team that went from 75 wins to 101 and nearly tripled its home attendance.

Ironically, owner Frank Navin had tried to hire one George Herman Ruth, better known as "Babe," as player-manager before the '34 season. After being offered the job, Ruth procrastinated and took a trip to Honolulu. Refusing to wait, Navin made a move he never regretted.

In 1935, Cochrane's last season as a full-time player, the Tigers slipped to 93 wins but drew more than one million fans for just the second time. More importantly, they won their first World Series, beating the Cubs in six games.

After a pair of second-place showings and a runner-up finish, Cochrane gave way to Del Baker as manager after five seasons. Cochrane's .582 winning percentage is tops in Detroit history, not counting two wins for Dick Tracewski and one for Billy Hitchcock in fill-in assignments.

Perhaps his success had something to do with the position he played. Of the Tigers' 36 managers, 11 have been major-league catchers. And that doesn't count Leyland, who caught 446 games in the minors, or Bill Freehan, who returned to Michigan as head baseball coach from 1990-1996.

But no one called the shots from the dugout and the pitches behind the plate like Cochrane—at least until beaned by Yankees pitcher Bump Hadley on May 25, 1937. A wayward fastball that No. 3 lost in the sun fractured his skull in three places, ended his playing career, and helped speed the move toward batting helmets.

"I should've worn a helmet that day in Yankee Stadium," Cochrane said a month later in Henry Ford Hospital. "It could've been worse. But I've caught my last game."

The pitch hit Cochrane so hard it left him in critical condition for two days and put a visible dent in his head. Six years earlier on a tour of Japan with American stars, Cochrane had been on the other end of an accident, homering into the front teeth of a fan. Japanese officials paid the man 50 yen to leave the park immediately and get false teeth.

Edward Mayo Smith played 73 games in the majors, batting .212 with no home runs for the 1945 Athletics. And there was nothing on his managerial record to shout "future world champion" when he came to Detroit in 1967.

After never winning more than 77 games with the Phillies from 1955-58 and being fired by the Reds at the 1959 All-Star break, Smith settled in as a scout for the Yankees from 1960-1966. At age 52, he got another opportunity and shocked the cynics.

His first try with the Tigers nearly produced a pennant. Instead, Detroit split back-to-back doubleheaders with the Angels to finish 91-71, one game behind the "Impossible Dream" Red Sox, led by Triple Crown winner Carl Yastrzemski.

Some suggested that Smith took smart pills the following year. And when someone scrawled "Let's win in spite of Mayo" on the wall in the tunnel in Tiger Stadium, it took a respected veteran like recently acquired third baseman Eddie Mathews to say, "I don't know who wrote it, but it better come down!"

The message vanished, but the team never did. Despite three straight losses to end the season, Detroit finished 103-59, 12 games better than the Orioles. "Mayo Who?" earned baseball's Manager of the Year Award for 1968 from *The Sporting News*. And the moment that separated him from all the other Smiths was yet to come.

By risking immense ridicule and shifting center fielder Mickey Stanley to shortstop for the '68 World Series, Smith was able to bench Ray "0-for-August" Oyler and get a healthy, hot Al Kaline back in right field. Jim Northrup moved to center and had the key triple in Game 7, making Smith seem brighter than he was.

"I don't think Mayo was a great manager," famed broadcaster Ernie Harwell said. "He was a good fellow hanging on. Most of the '68 Tigers said, 'Leave us alone. Don't bother us.' And I think the switch of Mickey to shortstop was very uncharacteristic of Mayo. It was an experiment I didn't think would work at all. Instead, it worked great."

Detroit dropped to 90 wins in 1969, when no team could have caught Baltimore—not until the Mets showed up in October. But when the Tigers tumbled to 79 wins the following year, Smith was out with a 363-285 record, .560 success in four seasons.

"The fans in Detroit know as much about baseball as Chinese aviators," he said in a parting shot, though the Mayo Smith Society lives on as the team's top fan club.

If Smith was a glass of warm milk, Alfred Manuel Martin was a double shot of whiskey—and bartender, keep 'em comin'!

His doting mother called him "Bello"—Italian for beautiful. And no one disputes the fact that Martin had one of the brightest minds in baseball, especially when he directed his remaining brain cells toward the field instead of the night's other activities.

But a self-destructive impulse took "Billy the Kid" down in less than three seasons. That decision was one of the few things Tigers general manager Jim Campbell and Yankees owner George Steinbrenner had in common.

"His first year he always did a great job," Kaline said. "But he was a tough guy to play for. It was very easy to get on his list—and that list starts with an 's'."

Martin was 1-1 in bouts with pitchers Dave Boswell and Ed Whitson. He also fought with two traveling secretaries, a fan outside Tiger Stadium, a cabbie in Chicago, a sportswriter in Reno, two bouncers in a topless bar, and a marshmallow salesman.

It was no great shock that alcohol was a major contributor when he died in a car crash on Christmas Day 1989.

"Billy was a good manager," Harwell said. "He was a smart strategist. He knew the game. And he managed with boldness.

He was a hunch player. But he had so many faults, they finally caught up with him. His need for vindication didn't do him any good. He had to get revenge all the time. We'd be waiting for the lineup, and Billy wasn't there. Finally, we'd get it. Tracewski would do it, or the other players would."

When Detroit lost five straight games, Martin had Kaline draw the batting order from a hat. Slugging first baseman Norm Cash hit leadoff. But the result was the same.

"Billy Martin might have been the best manager in baseball, but he wasn't with the Tigers," longtime *Detroit News* writer Jerry Green said. "He was volatile and angry. I wouldn't say he was inebriated before games. But I would say he indulged, because I saw that. He got into a flap with a fan in Baltimore and alibied his way out of it. I wrote a column, referring to him as 'Alibi Billy.' He was incensed. A day later, we were fine."

For every player who loved Martin, another one despised him. And what cost him his job wasn't a game that was lost—just the team's respect.

"Billy added six years to my career," left fielder Willie Horton said. "He came to my home when he took over the Tigers and said, 'You know what? You're a great ballplayer. But you're not going to play for me. You're going to get a lot of splinters. I can't have you going through the motions.' Billy took me to another level."

He also took credit for everything but sunshine. In the eyes of Northrup and other players, they were managed by Billy Martyr. When Detroit won, No. 1 was a genius. When they lost, he had a lot of bad ballplayers.

And some say two questionable moves—having Bill Freehan catch with a broken thumb and putting Duke Sims in left field against Oakland—cost the Tigers at least two games in the 1972 American League Championship Series.

Martin's teams were 253-208, a .549 success rate, in less than three full seasons with Detroit. But why did it seem so much longer than that? Perhaps for the same reason he lasted just one division-winning season in Minnesota, completed just one season

Detroit Tigers manager Sparky Anderson argues a call with umpire Tim McClelland. *(Photo by Andrew D. Bernstein/Getty Images)*

in Texas, and was hired and fired by the Yankees five times. Donald Trump didn't say, "You're fired!" that often in the first season of *The Apprentice*.

George Lee Anderson was fired just once—by Cincinnati in 1978 after two world championships, another World Series, and two division titles in nine seasons. The Tigers could never say "Thank you!" enough.

The winningest manager in Detroit history was 1.331-1,248—.516 success—from 1979-1995. His 1984 World Champions won 104 regular-season games. And his 1989 cellar-dwellers lost 103. No wonder Anderson understood a basic baseball truth, "Players decide games. Managers dissect them."

"That opened my eyes," the 2000 Hall of Famer and fourth-winningest manager in history said. "I realized then I wasn't king. I wasn't as great as I thought."

No. 11 often said a manager might make the difference in, at most, five games a year. That was true whether or not he stepped on the baseline on the way to the mound, as the super-superstitious Anderson refused to do.

But if Sparky-ese was an odd mix of malaprops and hyperbole, with Kirk Gibson the next Mickey Mantle and Chris Pittaro a future star, Anderson could communicate with players in a way few managers ever have.

Arguably his greatest player, Reds catcher Johnny Bench, said in *They Call Me Sparky*, Anderson's book with Dan Ewald: "A good manager will tell you there's more than one way to skin a cat. A great manager will convince the cat it's necessary. Sparky had the cats carrying knives to him."

"Sparky is a master manipulator," Green said. "And I mean that in a good way. I'd go into his office and say, 'I'm going to ask him why he did this or that in the fourth inning.' I'd leave talking about something in the ninth, never knowing what happened. He was the smartest man ever from South Dakota. Okay, there were two of them—Sparky and Tom Brokaw."

"When Sparky said the best manager can only make five games' difference, he was right about that," Harwell said. "A manager can't win the pennant for you. But he knew how to push the right buttons. And he had a strong sense of honor. He didn't care if you were from *The New York Times* or *The Podunk News.* He treated you the same."

Anderson refused to manage replacement players and walked away from the game during the strike of 1994. Some thought he should have done the job he was being paid to do. His principles said otherwise. He had lines he wouldn't cross.

CHAPTER THIRTEEN

The Bats

HEILMANN, KELL, KUENN-COLAVITO, AND FIELDER

THE BATS HAVE COME IN ALL SHAPES AND SIZES. So have the batters. But the fact remains, the Detroit Tigers have won more than twice as many American League batting titles as the New York Yankees. Even without Ty Cobb's greatness, Detroit would have a 10-9 advantage.

From 1921 to 1927 the Tigers won five batting crowns in seven seasons. That didn't include a .401 runner-up finish by Cobb in 1922. Instead, it was a decade when Harry Heilmann was "The Man," with four batting championships in odd-numbered seasons. And teammate Heinie Manush kept Heilmann's throne warm in 1926.

Twelve years after Charlie Gehringer had the league's top average in 1937, George Kell was king. And four seasons after Al Kaline was the youngest titlist at age 20 in 1955, Harvey Kuenn captured the crown. Kell and Kuenn shared another thing a decade apart. Each ended a two-year run by Ted Williams.

Before Kuenn could take his next at-bat, he was dealt to Cleveland for home run champion Rocky Colavito. But the only Tiger to lead the league in homers in back-to-back years was Cecil Fielder in 1990-1991. His 51 dingers in '90 were second in franchise history behind Hank Greenberg's 58 in '38.

Let's start with one of the most underrated players any sport has known, right fielder-first baseman Harry Edwin Heilmann. Only Cobb, Rod Carew, and Wade Boggs have led the American League in hitting more often. And no one in either league, not even Cobb, could say he won three or more titles and hit .393 or better every time.

Heilmann ranks second on Detroit's all-time list with a .343 batting average. His .342 career mark, including one season plus another 31 at-bats with Cincinnati, ranks 10th in major-league history—.002 behind Williams' numbers and the same as Babe Ruth's.

"I never saw him play but knew all about him," Hall of Fame voice and historian Ernie Harwell said. "To hit that close to .400 four times says an awful lot. He played for Cobb in the '20s and was overshadowed by Ruth, Lou Gehrig, and Jimmie Foxx. The averages were all inflated in those days. But to lead the league that often in that era was pretty good."

The San Francisco native improved immediately when Cobb became a player-manager. Heilmann's average soared from .309 in 1920 to .394 the following year—.005 higher than Cobb's runner-up effort. Heilman also led the league with a career-high 237 hits and finished second to Ruth with a .606 slugging percentage and 139 RBIs. More than just a slap hitter, Heilmann rapped 43 doubles, 14 triples, and 19 homers in 1921.

After "slumping" to .356 the next year, when he had a career-best 21 homers, a player known as "Slug" hit .403 in 1923, the 10th highest average of the 20th century and the highest for any Tiger since 1912.

A model of consistency, Heilmann hit .393 in 1925 and had 134 hits on the road, a record that stood for 79 years. And he hit .398 in 1927, when he beat Al Simmons of the A's with a 6-for-8 season-ending doubleheader. Heilmann finished one hit shy of reaching .400 again, though that performance was lost in Ruth's pursuit of 60 homers.

His other seasons weren't shabby, either. Heilmann hit .346 in 1924, .367 in 1926, and .344 in 1929. He had 12 straight years with at least a .300 average and 10 Top-10 finishes in American League batting. But his best contribution was off the field. On July 25, 1916, Heilmann dove into the Detroit River and saved the life of a drowning woman.

He was a bookkeeper when he was offered his first baseball job in 1913. And Heilmann made a smooth transition when arthritic wrists ended his career in 1932, just after he became the first player to homer in every major-league ballpark. For 17 seasons from 1934-1950, he was the Tigers' play-by-play voice on radio—and later on television.

Heilmann was a great storyteller, as Harwell noted. That was clear from his tale of the minister who scolded him for playing on Sundays. When the player pointed out that the minister worked on Sundays, too, the quick response was, "But I'm in the right field!" Without missing a beat, Heilmann said, "I am, too, and ain't that sun hell?"

Heilmann died of lung cancer in 1951 at age 56 and was elected to the Hall of Fame the following year. He ranked 54th in *The Sporting News' 100 Greatest Baseball Players.*

Another batting champ-turned-broadcaster, George Clyde Kell, got as much out of his natural gifts as anyone in the Hall of Fame. The pride of Swifton, Arkansas, played for five American League teams and wore five different numbers, including three—21, 15, and 7—in seven seasons as Detroit's third baseman.

Rejected by many as a marginal prospect, Kell continued to work at his craft and became a 10-time All-Star. The 5-foot-9, 175-pounder received more All-Star votes from the fans in 1950 than any player in either league. Kell also received considerable respect from his peers.

"He doesn't have the power of Joe DiMaggio or Ted Williams, but every time you look up, he's on base," Hall of Fame pitcher Ted Lyons said. "He drives you nuts."

Kell drove himself to be the best player he could be. And that was a very good one. He hit .396 at Class B Lancaster in 1943, the best mark in organized baseball, and debuted with the Philadelphia Athletics on the last day of that season. On May 18,

In June of 1950, third baseman George Kell springs toward first base after lashing out a sharp single. *(Photo by Hy Peskin/Time & Life Pictures/Getty Images)*

1946, he was dealt to the Tigers by Connie Mack's club for outfielder Barney McCosky.

"Mr. Mack called me in and said, 'George, I've traded you to Detroit,'" Kell recalled. "He said. 'I can't pay you. Detroit can.' And Detroit did. But everyone there treated me well. Even when I went 0-for-5 and got booed for the first time, Hank Greenberg came over and said, 'You've got it made now. They don't boo you here till you've been successful.'"

Kell was successful with the bat and the glove. A career .306 hitter, he batted over .300 nine times, including six straight years with the Tigers. Kell also led American League third basemen in fielding percentage seven times.

Perhaps the best example of the way he played came on August 29, 1948, in Yankee Stadium. Leading New York 2-1, Kell stopped a shot down the line by DiMaggio—with his face.

His jaw broken in two places, Kell somehow scooped up the ball and scrambled to third in time for a force out. His first words when he regained his senses were, "Did I get him out?"

He got the out on DiMaggio's blast and got a batting title that Williams thought he'd won the following year. With "Teddy Ballgame" 10 points ahead with 10 games left in 1949, the engraver was ready to work on Williams' fifth trophy and third in a row. Suddenly, everything changed.

Entering the final day of the season, Williams led .344-.341. With the Red Sox and Yankees tied for first place, Williams had to play. And he would've played anyway, as he did in '41 with a .400 season on the line. But when Williams popped out twice and walked twice, an 0-for-2 day dropped him to .3427562.

Meanwhile, Kell singled and doubled against starter Bob Lemon, then drew a walk off Bob Feller, who was on in relief. A flyout left him 2-for-3 and boosted his average to .3429119, just .0001567 ahead of Williams.

Kell was in the on-deck circle when teammate Eddie Lake bounced into a season-ending double play. But Detroit manager Red Rolfe knew the numbers and would have pinch hit, if necessary, to get the title—something Kell never knew until the off-season.

He still holds the record for the fewest strikeouts by a batting champ (13). And Kell never fanned more than 23 times in any of his first 11 major-league seasons.

In 1950 he made a run at back-to-back crowns, leading the league with 218 hits and 56 doubles. Kell wound up at .340, not counting his 14 innings in the All-Star Game. But Williams' teammate Billy Goodman hit .354 for Boston, 41 points higher than his next-best season.

Twenty months later Kell was shipped to the Red Sox in a nine-player deal. He finished his career with Chicago and Baltimore, where he was succeeded by an even-better gloveman from Arkansas, Brooks Robinson.

Kell began broadcasting games for the Orioles and CBS in 1957-1958. In 1959 he returned to the Tigers and spent the next

38 years at the mic. His 45 seasons with the Detroit organization rank with anyone except Al Kaline.

Kell's first year in the booth at Briggs Stadium was the last with the Tigers for Harvey Edward Kuenn, a shortstop-turned-outfielder. The 1953 American League Rookie of the Year played in eight straight All-Star Games with Detroit. Only Kaline (18) and catcher Bill Freehan (11) appeared there more often as Tigers.

Kuenn hit .314 in eight years with Detroit and .303 in 15 seasons overall. He had a career-high 209 hits in his first full season, including a major-league rookie record of 167 singles. Kuenn had 201 hits in 1954, led the league in that category and in doubles twice. His .353 average in '59 gave no clue of what was to follow—as a hard-partying player past his prime or as the manager of "Harvey's Wallbangers" in Milwaukee.

On April 17, 1960, the Sunday before the season began, the Tigers and Indians rocked the baseball world. Cleveland got Kuenn, while Detroit landed Rocco Domenico Colavito, a rocket-armed right fielder who'd clubbed 83 homers in 1958-1959.

"I was very surprised," Kaline said. "Harvey was a good friend of mine. And I did well when he was here because he was on base all the time. I got to drive in a lot of runs. But they called me in and said, 'Now, you get on base, and Rocky will drive you in.' It was a different mindset. But it turned out to be a great trade for the Tigers."

The deal was wildly unpopular in Ohio, where it's still being blamed for a 59-year championship drought in Terry Pluto's book *The Curse of Rocky Colavito*. Of course it didn't help that Indians general manager Frank Lane made it worse with his famous line, "What's all the fuss about? All I did was trade hamburger for steak."

If Colavito was hamburger, he must've been a double-meat Whopper in 1961. The Bronx native hit 45 homers and drove in 140 runs as the Tigers won 101 games and scared the Yanks for most of the season. By that point Kuenn had already been traded to San Francisco, where he did what Colavito couldn't—play in a World Series.

"They weren't a couple of Humpty Dumptys," Harwell said. "Harvey was a fine player but didn't take good care of himself. Rocky was in better condition. Harvey was a great hitter off his front foot and got a lot of singles. Colavito struck out a lot but hit for power and had a very strong arm—not as accurate as Al's, though."

Colavito switched from right field to left. But he was always an active volcano. The only question was when he'd erupt. He went into the stands in Yankee Stadium when his wife and father got into it with a drunken fan. And he went after then-*Free Press* columnist Joe Falls, who incorrectly charged him with an error and introduced the stat RNBI (runs NOT batted in) for the Tigers' new No. 7.

"His fans said, 'Don't knock 'The Rock!' and he was really a matinee idol, especially in Cleveland," Harwell said. "But he did all those calisthenics when he came to the plate. When Detroit played the Yankees in that game that went forever, Colavito came up in the 22nd inning and went into his stretching regimen. I remember Whitey Ford hollering, 'Rocky, aren't you loose yet?'"

Fans in the left-field seats in Tiger Stadium had to stay loose when their team signed slugging first baseman-designated hitter Cecil Grant Fielder from Hanshin in Japan's Central League—a Tigers-to-Tigers transaction before the 1990 season began.

Fielder's nickname went from "Wild Bear" in Japan to "Big Daddy" in Michigan. And his output jumped from 38 homers with Hanshin to 51 in Detroit, where he became the first player with 50 since George Foster socked 52 for Sparky Anderson's "Big Red Machine" in 1977.

The Tigers' gentle giant was listed at 6-foot-3, 250 pounds, though baseball historian Bill James said, "One must wonder what would happen if he put his other foot on the scale."

No one can quibble with Fielder's power numbers. No. 45 hit 44 homers in 1991 to claim back-to-back American League crowns. And he became the first player since Ruth in 1919-1921 to win three straight RBI titles, driving in 132, 133, and 124 runs from 1990-1992. It was just too bad he didn't have help.

"I always looked at Fielder as kind of a clown act," Detroit sportscaster Mark Wilson said. "We went to New York when he hit the 50th homer. But we weren't following the team, just him. It's funny, but I remember the day Fielder signed with the Tigers, they also signed Tony Bernazard to play second. And we thought that was a bigger signing. We were all calling him 'CEEE-cil Fielder.'"

No one was calling him late for dinner. But he was edged in MVP voting by Rickey Henderson in 1990 and Cal Ripken Jr. the following year. And from 1990-1995, including a strike-shortened season in '94, no one hit more home runs than Fielder's 219.

"Some people can hit things. Other people can't," said ex-Detroit slugger Willie Horton. "As far as where all your power comes from, I don't think you can teach power. I think you've got to be born with it. I think you can teach consistency. But the great power hitters are born with power."

Too much economic power led to serious problems for Fielder. Despite a reported $47 million in career salary, gambling cost him a marriage and a 50-room mansion in Melbourne, Florida. He once lost $580,000 in a 40-hour freefall at Trump Plaza in Atlantic City, New Jersey.

But when he was good, he was great. Like Heilmann, Kell, Kuenn and, yes, Colavito, when Fielder was right, he wasn't just steak. He was baseball's filet mignon.

CHAPTER FOURTEEN

The Arms

NEWHOUSER, BUNNING, LOLICH, MORRIS, AND JONES

LONG BEFORE THEY HAD THE BEST EARNED-RUN AVERAGE and the most shutouts in the majors in 2006, the Detroit Tigers had tremendous pitchers. American League batters would tell you they still do.

From George Mullin, "Hooks" Dauss, "Schoolboy" Rowe, and Tommy Bridges in the first half of the 20th century to Frank Lary, Denny McLain, John Hiller, and Willie Hernandez in the past 50 years, the Olde English "D" often stood for dominance.

But five pitchers—four starters and a closer—deserve special recognition. Two are in the Hall of Fame. Two more might be. And one is the Tigers' career saves leader, at least until Joel Zumaya gets five or six seasons in that role.

A team could hang a string of American League pennants with Hal Newhouser, Jim Bunning, Mickey Lolich, and Jack Morris—a lefty-righty-lefty-righty rotation that would lower a lot of batting averages. But whatever you do, don't tell Morris that he's the fourth starter. In the postseason he wouldn't be.

And to finish games, who better than Todd Jones? So what if he stranded more runners than a faulty starter's pistol in the *Free Press* Marathon? They don't judge saves like skating routines. All they do is count them.

The ace of the staff would be Harold Newhouser, a homegrown hero who signed in 1939 and was a winning pitcher at age 18. But with a 34-50 record in his first four full seasons in Detroit, no one could have guessed what would come next from an immature player who asked to be traded just before his breakthrough season.

"His temper was a problem for a while," legendary broadcaster and baseball historian Ernie Harwell said. "But (catcher) Paul Richards calmed him down and taught him the slider. Hal got into the Hall of Fame late. A lot of people thought his numbers were inflated because of when he played. He had some very good years after World War II, though. And you can make the case that Hal was the best the Tigers have had."

He was also the game's biggest eater. According to mound mate "Dizzy" Trout, the 6-foot-2, 192-pound Newhouser once won a bet by downing 14 steak sandwiches, three barbecue chicken sandwiches, and two quarts of ice cream at one sitting— truly a Ruthian effort. When he finally stopped chewing, he said that was only because he didn't want to make a pig of himself.

Just as hungry for victories, "Prince Hal" won 188 games before his 30th birthday, more than any pitcher in the live-ball era. He had five more Ws in his teens and 20s than "Catfish" Hunter and nine more than Robin Roberts.

Newhouser was the American League MVP in 1944, going 29-9 with a 2.22 ERA and a league-high 187 strikeouts. He repeated as MVP the following season and posted a 25-9 mark, a 1.81 ERA and 212 Ks, plus a second World Series win in Game 7. And with everyone back from the war in '46, Newhouser went 26-9 with a 1.94 ERA and a career-high 275 strikeouts, finishing second to Ted Williams in the MVP voting.

"When you talk about the Tigers' rotation in heaven, I think you have to start with Newhouser," *ESPN Baseball Encyclopedia* editor Gary Gillette said. "Some still say his greatness was partly achieved in wartime. But you can't overlook his numbers."

No. 16 wasn't the only Detroit player to be classified 4-F by his draft board. Though he attempted to enlist several times, he was always rejected. And '46 wasn't Newhouser's only good year in peacetime. He won 56 games from 1947-1949, including a league-best 21 in '48. Included was a 4-1 victory over the A's on June 15, 1948, the first night game in Briggs Stadium.

When the Tigers let Newhouser go after the 1953 season, he signed as a reliever with Cleveland and played a key role for another American League champ. His career numbers: 207-150 with a 3.06 ERA and 1,796 strikeouts.

After becoming a bank vice president and a scout for Baltimore, he found pitcher Milt Pappas, who won 209 games. And with Houston he was credited with discovering shortstop Derek Jeter, though the Astros passed on him in favor of catcher Phil Nevin.

James Paul David Bunning, better known as Senator Jim Bunning from the Commonwealth of Kentucky, pitched for Detroit for nine seasons from 1955-1963. He spent eight more years with Philadelphia, Pittsburgh, and Los Angeles in the National League.

Bunning's no-hitter in Boston on July 20, 1958, was the fourth in Tigers history. And he celebrated Father's Day in 1964 with a perfect game for the Phillies against the Mets, the National League's first in 84 years. That made No. 14 one of just five men to throw a no-hitter in each league.

The 6-3 Bunning would fall off the mound toward first base on most deliveries. That didn't stop him from becoming a seven-time All-Star, five with Detroit and two with Philadelphia after being dealt for Don Demeter.

His breakthrough season came in 1957 at age 25, when he led the league in wins, went 20-8, and compiled a 2.69 ERA. Bunning became the fifth American League pitcher to strike out the side on nine pitches against the Red Sox in 1959. He led the American League in strikeouts in 1959-1960 with 201 each time, then went 17-11 with a 2.79 ERA in 1961 and 19-10 in '62.

Bunning was elected to the Hall of Fame by the Veterans Committee 25 years after his final pitch. By the time he was enshrined, he had received well over 3,000 votes for the Hall, more than any player in history. And none of those votes were from people he had helped in the formation of the Major League Baseball Players Association.

"Bunning didn't particularly care for us," longtime *Detroit News* sportswriter Jerry Green said. "Frank Lary would beat the Yankees all the time, and I always felt Bunning was intimidated by the Yankees. But a year or two before he was elected, he finally came back to Tiger Stadium. I said, 'Jim, I'm voting for you for the Hall of Fame.' He said, 'Thank you.' That was it."

His political career began with a seat on the city council in Fort Thomas, Kentucky. After being elected to the Kentucky Senate, Bunning was defeated as the Republican candidate for governor in 1983. Three years later he was elected to Congress, where he served six two-year terms. In 1998 he switched to the U.S. Senate, where he was most visible in its steroids probe.

In April 2006 he was selected by *Time* magazine as one of "America's Five Worst Senators," where it was stated that he "shows little interest in policy unless it involves baseball." Eight months later Bunning was on the losing side of a 95-2 vote to confirm Robert Gates as Secretary of Defense—the equivalent of a 10-run first inning.

Michael Stephen Lolich put donuts on the scoreboard for the better part of 16 seasons. Then, he put them into the hands of some hungry customers at his shop in Lake Orion, Michigan.

A Tiger from 1963-1975, Lolich was a model of durability and consistency—though never one of fashion or fitness. He still holds franchise records with 459 starts, 39 shutouts, and 2,679 strikeouts—"Paunch-out Punchouts," as one writer described them.

Lolich will long be remembered for outdueling St. Louis great Bob Gibson in Game 7 of the 1968 World Series, a 4-1 Detroit win in Busch Stadium. With his efforts in Games 2 and 5, that short-rest masterpiece made him the last man to pitch three complete-game victories in one Series.

"My arm was pretty dead," Lolich said. "But Mayo Smith said, 'All I need is five innings.' Then, it was, 'Can you give me six?' … 'How about seven?' The ball kept sinking. And I was hitting the corners. No one even warmed up in the bullpen."

Lolich was hot enough to heat a small city. He even hit the only homer of his 16-year major-league career in Game 2, giving him one in 840 at-bats. No wonder a lover of Kawasaki motorcycles drove off with a new Corvette as the Series MVP.

"I don't think Mickey gets the credit that he deserves for being a great pitcher," Al Kaline said. "There's always one guy that you don't score many runs for, and Lolich was that guy on our team. Yet, he went on and had a great career—a Hall of Fame career, I think. But he had to battle all the time."

That struggle began at age two when his tricycle hit a parked motorcycle. The bike fell on top of Lolich and broke his left collarbone in two spots. Exercises developed his left arm to unique levels. But Lolich did everything else right-handed and was one of the few players to throw left-handed and bat—or at least try to—the other way.

He didn't begin playing baseball until age 12 in Portland, Oregon. That late start must have carried over to Lolich's game preparation. No. 29 never liked to arrive at the park until an hour before he threw his first pitch. Once he did, he could go forever.

In 1971 Lolich went 376 innings, the most since Grover Cleveland Alexander 55 years earlier. He led the league with 25 wins, 29 complete games, and 308 strikeouts, and had a 2.92 ERA. But he was second to Oakland's Vida Blue in Cy Young Award voting.

In 16 seasons, including long cups of coffee with the Mets and Padres, Lolich won 217 games, had a 3.44 ERA, and fanned 2,832 hitters, No. 1 among southpaws at the time. Today Lolich ranks third among lefties, behind Randy Johnson and Steve Carlton.

"I don't think Mickey will make it into the Hall, though he probably should," Harwell said. "Denny McLain grabbed the headlines. But Mickey was a workhorse. He could work in the bullpen if you needed him to do that. What people remember is the '68 Series. There's no one pitching today who could've done that."

John Scott Morris could have come close. In 14 seasons with the Tigers and 18 years overall, he saved his best for the biggest games and his worst for the media. That constant friction could cost the best pitcher of the 1980s a spot in the Hall of Fame, at least until he gets to the Veterans Committee.

Morris won 198 games with the Tigers and 254 overall. He set a major-league record for pitchers with 13 straight Opening Day starts between 1980-1992 and made 490 appearances without missing a turn. What he missed was the adoration he felt he deserved. In part, that came from two media strikes when he felt particularly wronged.

"They've invaded my privacy," Morris said. "I have no time for myself or my family. From now on I'm not talking. I know I won't be misquoted."

Misquoted? No. Mistaken? Yes, especially in comments to female reporters. Perhaps that's why he never got full credit for five All-Star Game appearances, four with Detroit. He never finished higher than third in Cy Young Award voting, despite 233 wins from 1979-1992—41 more than anyone else. And he never got much hype from a 4-0 no-hitter in Chicago on April, 7, 1984.

"Jack has acknowledged the fact that he wasted a lot of time being a jerk," Gillette said. "He had a great career, a Hall of Fame career in my book. But he was very thin-skinned. If he hadn't been, he'd be in the Hall, even with a high ERA (3.90)."

"Mt. Morris" was booed in Tiger Stadium BEFORE the first start of his career. When it was announced that fan favorite Mark Fidrych couldn't go due to injury, the crowd took it out on Morris, who promptly earned his first career win.

The St. Paul, Minnesota, native and former BYU Cougar finished with three more Ws than Gibson, 30 more than Bunning, 45 more than Hunter and Don Drysdale, and 89 more than Sandy Koufax.

And his success in October ranks with anyone's. Morris was a key player for four World Series winners—Detroit in 1984, Minnesota in 1991, and Toronto in 1992-93. He was 6-1 in postseason play, highlighted by 10 shutout innings in a Game 7 win over Atlanta in '91, when he was named the World Series MVP.

Overall, it was quite the ride—exhilarating but bumpy for a guy whose first pout came in his early years with the Tigers, when he ran into a minor-league rock named Jim Leyland.

"Jack was sent down to Triple-A and didn't want to be there," broadcaster Mario Impemba said. "He said Leyland told him to stop being a crybaby, to get his act together, get back to the big leagues, and never come back. That's exactly what happened."

No. 47 gave up some runs and his fair share of solo homers. But Morris pitched as well as he had to with a game on the line. And so has someone else—Detroit's career saves leader, despite testing pacemakers all over Michigan.

Todd Barton Givin Jones hasn't given in often in recording 263 saves, including 179 in two stints and 5 ⅔ seasons with the Tigers. Yes, his 3.95 ERA is ridiculously high for a closer. No, it hasn't stopped him from getting the ball to begin the ninth.

Jones shared the American League lead with a career-best 42 saves in 2000, becoming the first Detroit closer to win the Rolaids Relief Man of the Year Award. And he has saved 30 games five times, four with the Tigers. Hernandez is the only other Tiger to do it twice.

Still, the crowds at Comerica Park cringe if Jones gives up so much as a weak single with a three-run lead. That's okay with No. 59 as long as his manager isn't leading the groans. And with Leyland's confidence, Jones saved 37 games in 2006, his first season back with Detroit.

"It feels good because that's what I came here to do," Jones said. "I appreciate Jim's confidence in me. And I want to prove that his hunch was right. So far I've been able to do that."

Jones was able to do something else on September 27, 1999. He became the answer to the trivia question, "Who threw the last pitch in Tiger Stadium?" For the record, it was a strikeout of Kansas City outfielder and ex-Tiger Kimera Bartee at 7:07 p.m.

Somewhere, Newhouser, Bunning, Lolich, and even Morris had to be smiling.

CHAPTER FIFTEEN

The Gloves

FREEHAN, STANLEY, AND TRAMMELL-WHITAKER

FOR 11 DECADES, the Detroit Tigers have been blessed with some amazing fielders. And we're not talking about Cecil here.

Pick a position, and the franchise has enjoyed one of the top glovemen in baseball history. In many cases it had more than one of the best defenders the game has known.

From Ty Cobb, No. 5 in career putouts among outfielders and No. 2 in assists, to Kenny Rogers and Ivan Rodriguez, last season's Gold Glove battery, defense and Detroit have never been too far apart in the dictionary.

Before Rawlings introduced its award for fielding excellence in 1957, the Tigers had infielders who set the standard of excellence, whether their gloves were black, brown, orange, or gold.

Second baseman Charlie Gehringer and third baseman George Kell were walking clinics for how to play those positions. Both batting champs and Hall of Famers led the league in fielding percentage seven times.

Over the past half-century, 13 Detroit players have won a total of 38 Gold Gloves. And that's only counting two of Rodriguez's 12 cherished trophies, the pair he earned with a "D" on his cap.

Rodriguez's collection ranks first among backstops and is exceeded only by the 16 of third baseman Brooks Robinson and pitcher Jim Kaat, the 14 of pitcher Greg Maddux, and the 13 of shortstop Ozzie Smith.

The Tigers' leader in Gold Gloves is Al Kaline with 10. But then, who else had a spot in right field named for him? No. 6 did with "Kaline's Corner." He developed his arm by firing rocks at the "O" in speeding B&O freight trains. And at age 18, he had three outfield assists in one game—one at second, one at third, and one at home.

Catcher Bill Freehan is second with five Gold Gloves, followed by center fielder Mickey Stanley and shortstop Alan Trammell with four. Second baseman Lou Whitaker and catcher Lance Parrish have three, centerfielder Gary Pettis two, and pitcher Frank Lary and second baseman Frank Bolling one each.

That list doesn't include terrific fielders like first baseman Norm Cash, shortstops Ray Oyler and Ed Brinkman, and third basemen Don Wert and Aurelio Rodriguez.

Each had his own peculiarities. And no one had a stranger routine than Brinkman, who used to break in his gloves by pouring hot coffee on them. Cream and sugar, anyone? Either way, the cream of the American League set a major-league record with just seven errors in 1972 and a string of 72 straight errorless games.

But for a closer look at four of the best, let's start with William Ashley Freehan, who grew up near 12 Mile and Woodward in Royal Oak and hitchhiked or took the bus to Briggs Stadium. It was a short walk from his stop to Michigan and Trumbull.

As a sophomore at Michigan, Freehan was a starting end and linebacker in football and a triple-crown winner in baseball, batting .585 to set a Big Ten record. That led to a $100,000 bonus-baby contract in 1961, a rarity with the Tigers.

Still trying to earn his stripes with the veterans, Freehan split time behind the plate in Detroit with Gus Triandos in 1963, then caught 141 games in '64, when he had 20 home runs, 80 RBIs, and a career-high .300 average.

The sturdy 6-foot-3, 205-pounder began a string of 10 straight American League All-Star appearances and 11 mid-summer invitations in 12 years in 1965.

As great as he was at handling pitchers, and he was recognized by Rawlings as the best in the league from 1966-1970, Freehan wouldn't have had nearly the impact he did if he hadn't been such a factor on offense.

"Bill was an excellent catcher for a long, long time," Hall of Fame broadcaster Ernie Harwell said. "He and Lance Parrish were similar that way. Bill was an excellent handler of pitchers. And he could hit a homer for you."

Freehan had 20 home runs, 74 RBIs, and league-highs of 15 intentional walks and 20 hit-by-pitches in 1967, finishing third behind Boston's Carl Yastrzemski and Minnesota's Harmon Killebrew in the MVP race.

With career-highs of 25 homers, 84 RBIs, and 24 hit-by-pitches, the most plunks in the American League since 1911, Freehan was great the next year, too. He finished second to teammate Denny McLain, a 31-game winner, in the MVP balloting.

But we're talking about fielding here, and no one made a bigger play in the '68 World Series than Freehan when, with the Tigers on the brink of elimination, he blocked home plate to retire St. Louis jet Lou Brock in Game 5.

"It took a perfect throw from Willie Horton in left to get him," Freehan said. "Lou didn't respect Willie's arm the way he should have. I blocked the plate. And after the collision he tried to touch the plate again. That's when I tagged him a second time."

Freehan retired with major-league records for putouts, chances, and fielding percentage. His .993 career mark is the sixth highest of all-time and the second-best in American League history. He also has the highest percentage of solo home runs (68.0) of any player with at least 200 dingers.

Mitchell Jack Stanley didn't create as many runs as he prevented from 1964-1978. Patrolling a cavernous center field with 440-foot dimensions in Detroit, he became the first of just four every-day outfielders in history to have multiple error-free seasons.

"Stanley was as good a center fielder as you'll ever see," Harwell said of a player who was perfect in 1968 and '70. "I saw Mays and Mantle. Jimmy Piersall was great in center. DiMaggio was, too. And Stanley could hold his own with any of them. In later years, after he was hurt, he didn't have a good arm. But he could catch anything."

Including ground balls. Before every game Stanley would take infield practice to relieve tension, never knowing he'd soon field grounders on October afternoons in the most pressurized situation imaginable.

As the Tigers prepared for a World Series showdown with mighty St. Louis, baseball's defending champion, manager Mayo Smith had two concerns. Could he win when Oyler and backup shortstop were hitting .135 and .203, respectively? And how could he get a healthy Kaline in the lineup when Horton, Stanley, and Jim Northrup were as solid as any outfield in the majors?

How could he not do that? And the best solution was to make good use of Stanley's versatility, as seen every day before games.

"He always took infield and threw the ball around, just like a little kid," Kaline remembered. "We all agreed. And he did a great job. He knew that one mistake could cost us a world championship."

Most of the media laughed at the concept. A few had scathing columns half-written. But when Brock led off the bottom of the first in Game 1 with a grounder to short, just as he'd planned, No. 24 fielded the ball cleanly. He gunned it to first for the first of Detroit's 186 putouts in seven games.

"I had no idea the move would happen until about a week before the season ended," Stanley said. "Norm Cash always used to say I could play there. But I worried about what people would say if it didn't work and cost the team the Series. There was tremendous pressure. I didn't enjoy it. And fielding that first ball was big. When I made the throw to first to get Brock, I nearly broke Cash's hand."

Before games he would wrestle with Horton, who loved Stanley—also known as "Squirrelly"—like a brother from another mother. Maybe that relationship reflected a new dynamic on the streets of Detroit, at least while there was a championship to win.

That title happened in large part because one Gold Glove center fielder handled 32 chances at shortstop, turned three double plays, and made just two errors—meaningless lapses in 8-1 and 13-1 wins. Meanwhile, National League recipient Curt Flood misplayed Northrup's shot to center into a two-run triple in Game 7.

Stanley played 101 games in the outfield and 59 at shortstop for the Tigers in 1969. The next year he returned to center field full time and made it three straight Gold Gloves with 132 error-free games.

The Grand Rapids native ranks No. 10 among major-league outfielders with a .991 fielding percentage and made the Michigan Sports Hall of Fame with a .248 career batting average. Ah, the power of glove!

On September 9, 1977, near the end of an otherwise-forgettable 74-88 season, manager Ralph Houk wrote the names of Whitaker and Trammell on a Detroit lineup card for the first time. After 1,918 games, an American League record for any teammates, not just double-play combinations, they finally turned their last 6-4-3.

"Trammell and Whitaker were like one person covering two positions," Harwell said. "Lou was great on the double-play pivot. And after he matured he was probably the best hitter on the team. Alan loved to play the game. For Lou it was just a job. Sometimes he wouldn't take batting practice at all."

Alan Stuart Trammell came from Southern California. Louis Rodman Whitaker was born in Brooklyn. That was just the start of their differences. They didn't socialize a lot—and didn't have to. Mutual respect made all the difference for "Tramaker."

They slapped the ball the other way in their early years and slammed it into the seats when they matured. Their combined totals: 2,617 runs, 4,734 hits, 832 doubles, 130 triples, 429 homers, 2,087 RBIs, and 379 steals—plus seven Gold Gloves and 11 All-Star appearances.

"I get mad every time I think that there's a Hall of Fame without 'Tram' and 'Sweet Lou,'" Horton said. "There shouldn't even be a vote. They should be automatic."

In 1983 they became the first keystone combo with .300 averages since Luke Appling and Cass Michaels each did that for the '49 White Sox. And if Trammell and Whitaker weren't quite the equal of Cal Ripken Jr. and Joe Morgan, they were close enough to make opponents say, "Not those two again!"

"I'm proud to say that I played my entire career in Detroit," Trammell said. "That's a real compliment. And it was great to play next to a guy like Lou. We did some pretty good things."

Trammell, not Game 5 hero Kirk Gibson, was the MVP of the 1984 World Series. The 6-foot, 175-pounder hit .450,

Alan Trammell (left) and Lou Whitaker meet at second base during spring training in March of 1985. *(Photo by Andrew D. Bernstein/Getty Images)*

clubbed a pair of homers off Eric Show—both with Whitaker on base—in Game 4 and finished with a slugging percentage of .800.

Three years later Trammell had his career year, leading Detroit past Toronto for the division title. He scored 109 runs, had 205 hits, collected 34 doubles, 28 homers and 105 RBIs, batted .343, and was successful on 21 of 23 steal attempts. Somehow, he was edged by Blue Jays outfielder George Bell for the MVP award.

But as Darrell Evans took Frank Tanana's underhand flip for the final out in a 1-0 division-clinching win on the final day of the regular season, Whitaker dashed toward second base. He pulled the bag up, stanchion and all, for a Sweet souvenir—a gift from No. 1 to No. 3.

In the cluhouse that makeshift trophy was presented—one that meant as much as anything the league could've given:

2B This year's MVP
Alan Trammell
Congratulations
Louis Rodman Whitaker

Whitaker didn't have to take a backseat to Trammell or anyone else. He had a 68-game errorless streak, led American League second basemen in fielding percentage twice, showed the arm of the third baseman he once was and supplied a great blend of grace and power.

If anything, Whitaker made it look too easy. Some believe he should've had 350 home runs, not 244. Others point to the nonchalance that allowed him to forget to pack his uniform for the 1985 All-Star Game. Making due with replica gear, Whitaker wore an adjustable mesh hat and scrawled a "1" on the back of his jersey with a black marker.

That hasn't marred his accomplishments. In 1986, Whitaker was part of the first infield with four 20-homer hitters (with Evans, Trammell, and Darnell Coles). And he joined Rogers Hornsby and Morgan as the only second basemen to score 1,000 runs, drive in 1,000, collect 2,000 hits, and blast 200 homers.

"In my Hall of Fame, Whitaker is in, no question," Gillette said. "He isn't in the same wing of the Hall as Gehringer or Hornsby. He's not in the Immortal Wing or the All-Time Greats Wing. He's in what I call the Perennial All-Stars Wing. Believe me, there are a helluva lot worse players than Lou Whitaker in the Hall of Fame."

That's where "I-Rod" is headed—to the All-Time Greats Wing. Rodriguez is one of just four players with 10 Gold Gloves and a batting average of .300 or better, joining Willie Mays, Roberto Clemente, and Roberto Alomar. He threw out 44.1 percent of would-be base-stealers in 2005, then broke his own team record with 45.1 percent.

If Rodriguez didn't erase a runner, there was always a shot that Rogers would. His 86 pickoffs from the slab are second only to Mark Langston's 91 in baseball history.

But they weren't the only Tigers to win with defense in 2006. No one made more amazing plays at third or played with more abandon on foul pops near the stands than Brandon Inge. No one gave up his body like second baseman Placido Polanco in a game-saving, season-shortening catch in short center in Boston. And no one had a better day than Craig Monroe, who threw out three runners from left field in one game.

Gold-ness gracious! Their glove work was almost Kalinesque.

CHAPTER SIXTEEN

The Sights and Sounds

FAVORITE VENUES, UNIFORMS, AND VOICES

EVERYONE REMEMBERS THE FIRST TIME. It only happens once. The anticipation. The build-up. Finally, the sweet release of emotion. It's an experience you never forget.

That's how Detroit diehards describe their initial visit to Briggs/Tiger Stadium, a baseball shrine that can be ripped to shreds but never torn from our minds and hearts.

From the lush, green grass and dark-green seats to the clean, classic, navy-and-white home uniforms—arguably the best look in baseball—millions of preteens were introduced to our national pastime at the corner of Michigan and Trumbull—or simply "The Corner" to its closest friends.

Actually, there has been professional baseball in "The Motor City" as far back as 1881, when the Detroit Wolverines began an eight-year stay in the National League. They played their games at Recreation Park and even won a world championship in 1887, beating the St. Louis Browns of the American Association 10-5 in a sparsely attended 15-game series that moved about the country.

When Detroit debuted in the upstart American League in 1901, it brought along a nickname first attached by an unknown headline writer in the *Detroit Free Press* on April 16, 1895. "Strouthers' Tigers Showed Up Very Nicely" was the banner for a game story. And a string of related items was titled "Notes of the Detroit Tigers of 1895." The word "Tigers" never appeared in the text of either piece.

Baseball historians have long credited Phillip J. Reid, city editor of the *Detroit Evening News*, with inventing the name in 1896. Detroit manager George Stallings also took credit, saying his players' stockings had black-and-brown stripes that reminded fans of tiger markings.

Richard Bak's book, *A Place for Summer: A Narrative History of Tiger Stadium*, said the city had a military unit called the Detroit Light Guard—also known as "The Tigers"—dating back to the Civil War. When the club sought and received permission from the Light Guard to use that trademark in 1901, the Detroit Tigers were officially born.

The first 11 Tigers teams played their games at Bennett Park, an 8,500-seat facility at the state's most famous intersection. After three straight pennants from 1907-1909, the capacity grew to 14,000 in 1910.

But owner Frank Navin had other ideas. Thus, Navin Field opened for play on the same site on April 20, 1912—the same day as Boston's Fenway Park. The biggest difference from Bennett Park, other than seating for 23,000, was a 90-degree clockwise twist of the field. That put the right-field foul pole, not home plate, closest to the Michigan-and-Trumbull crosswalks.

Detroit's most famous sports facility was renamed Briggs Stadium in 1938, two years after Walter Briggs bought the team. As its capacity more than doubled, peaking with an overflow crowd of 58,369 for a doubleheader with the Yankees in 1947, its charm grew proportionately.

Where else would Babe Ruth's 700th home run clear the then-single-decked stands in right and roll down a street until it stopped some 800 feet from home plate, only to be bought back by "The Bambino" for the princely sum of $20?

Where else would we find the odd but effective outfield dimensions—340 feet down the line in left, 365 feet in left-center, 440 to straightaway center, 370 to right center, and 325 down the line in right?

Where else would we have a massive flagpole—125 feet high—in the field of play, just to the left of dead-center at the deepest part of the park, and a 10-foot-overhang of the warning track for the upper deck in right?

Where else would its team have to play all day games because it didn't have lights until 1948, making it the last American League stadium to have night baseball—and the second-to-last in either league, ahead of only Chicago's Wrigley Field?

Where else would 18-year-old Al Kaline be denied entry to a park by security guards who didn't believe he was a player, then perform so well that an area of the field and a section of the stands forever became known as "Kaline's Corner?"

Where else would the fans seated closest to the foul lines be able to taunt or touch relief pitchers, with both bullpens in play and a lookout required to save players warming up from foul balls?

Where else would we see fights with Joe Louis and Jake LaMotta, the Detroit Lions' 1935, 1953, and 1957 NFL Championship wins—the latter a 59-14 trouncing of Cleveland—and baseball's 1941, 1951, and 1971 All-Star Games?

Where else would you find upper- and lower-deck bleachers in the outfield, obstructed-view seats in almost every section, a third deck in the outfield in right, and a giant transformer on the roof in right center that kept Reggie Jackson's blast in the '71 All-Star Game from orbiting the earth?

Where else could you see players sweat and hear them swear or have a visiting player tell Ernie Harwell he could hear his broadcast from center field?

Where else would the movie *61** —the story of the 1961 New York Yankees and Roger Maris' record-breaking 61 home runs— be shot 39 years later?

And where else would '61 Yankees catcher Yogi Berra be confused by the sign:

VISITORS CLUBHOUSE
NO VISITORS ALLOWED

Only at Briggs Stadium from 1938-1960 and Tiger Stadium from 1961-1999.

"Oh, what great memories!" Kaline said. "I remember thinking, 'I'm playing on the same field that Cobb and Gehringer and Greenberg did.' The place was so rich in tradition. And the fans in Detroit loved it more than the players."

As much as Tigers owner Mike Ilitch loved the memories, he understood the economic realities. Emotions aside, he weighed the merits of an impractical restoration attempt and the construction of a 21st-century facility.

Thus, despite the pleas and the plans of the Tiger Stadium Fan Club, the decision was made to leave Corktown for Foxtown and a publicly financed $300 million ballpark, with Comerica Bank agreeing to pay $66 million for 30 years of naming rights.

Saying goodbye has been particularly tough for Detroit native Willie Horton, who grew up playing Strikeout against the outer walls of the stadium and came up big when his team and his town needed him most in the 1968 World Series.

But after a six-year get-acquainted period when the bells and whistles meant more than Tigers homers that whistled into the seats, Comerica Park became relevant in 2006. Some have suggested the concrete and steel began to have soul. But that's what dramatic homers and pennant winners will do.

Initially, some suggested the name should have been Comerica National Park, as spacious as the outfield dimensions were. But when the bullpens were moved from right field to left and the left-field fences were brought in, the new dimensions— 345, 370, 420, 365, and 330 from left to right—weren't much different from Tiger Stadium's.

Players and media appreciated the improved working conditions. And fans enjoyed the modern comforts of Comerica, with a capacity of 41,070, especially when it seemed that everyone had to use a restroom at roughly the same time. Overall, they had choices and conveniences they never would have had at Tiger Stadium.

Tradition can't be bought or created overnight. And Comerica Park can't create the magic in seven years that "The Corner" did in 88 seasons. But the memories of 2006 were a good place to start. You know that when an eight-year-old leaves his first game and says to his or her parents, 'That was really fun! Did you come here when you were a kid?'"

One thing that hasn't changed appreciably is a distinctive navy-and-white home ensemble, with thin blue trim from neck to knees, a hat that's worn from Hollywood to Hong Kong, and an olde English "D" that immediately shouts "DETROIT TIGERS."

Actually, there are different calligraphic D's—the team logo that has appeared on the left breast of the uniform for generations and a variation that shows up on the cap and the grass behind home plate.

The official logo has a rounded upper-right corner, three descending strokes—two straight and one wavy—and two evenly spaced, rounded connecters from the third bar to the letter's right edge. The alternative "D" has two more angular peaks at the upper-right corner, just two descendants—both curved—and closer connecters with opposite slopes.

But the look and the smells of Tigers baseball aren't the only impressions on our senses. Thousands of sight-impaired fans have followed the team for decades and felt as involved as anyone with a front-row season ticket.

The first great voice of Detroit baseball appropriately was named Ty. Just as Ty Cobb was leaving the Tigers, the legendary Ty Tyson stepped into the radio booth in 1927 and stayed through the 1942 season—for home games only. He returned as the lead voice on Detroit's first local telecast team from 1947-1952 and came back for one more year of radio, home and away, in 1951.

Hall of Fame outfielder Harry Heilmann made a seamless transition from the batter's box to the broadcast booth from 1934-1952, doing radio for the first 17 seasons and moving to TV for the final six, including a four-year overlap.

Heilmann's partner in 1949, "The Ol' Announcer" himself, Van Patrick, took over as a solo act in 1952, then worked with Dizzy Trout, Mel Ott, and George Kell from 1953-1959 on radio and television.

It was Patrick who coined the phrase "Sunday Punch" to describe Charlie Maxwell's propensity for homers on the Sabbath.

And it was Kell who paved the way for Harwell to come to Detroit from Baltimore, after stints with the Dodgers and Giants. Let's just let "The Voice of Summer" tell the tale. As Harwell might say, just sit back and take it all in like "the house by the side of the road."

"I knew George toward the end of his playing career, when I was doing Orioles games," Harwell said. "In '57 he'd been injured a lot. And one day he came up to the booth to see how good the ice cream was. We asked him to do a half-inning, and he really enjoyed it. Then he got a job with CBS, doing the pregame show, and started doing the games in Detroit with Van Patrick in '59. At the end of the year, he called me and said, 'Van's not coming back. I think the Tigers would like to have you. Would you be interested?' I said that I would be, and that's what happened."

Kell and Harwell did radio and TV as a tandem from 1960-1963, then went different ways until Kell retired in 1996 and Harwell's third stint ended in 2002, when "a lady from Livonia" caught a foul ball for the last time. No one has ever had a better sense of where every fan lived or made life away from the ballpark more fun.

Harwell also had a story or two million to tell along the way. And one of the best involved himself, when he left the booth after being told a game was rained out. He was on the freeway heading home with his wife, Lulu, when he heard Ray Lane pleading over

Tigers radio broadcaster Ernie Harwell waves to the Detroit crowd during the seventh-inning stretch in a game against the New York Yankees on September 22, 2002. *(Photo by Carlos Osorio/AFP/Getty Images)*

the air, "Come back, Ernie!" Tigers president Jim Campbell wasn't laughing.

The Hall of Famer and signature voice of a state worked with former manager Bob Scheffing and broadcast sidekicks Gene Osborne, Lane, the great Paul Carey for 19 years, Rick Rizzs, Bob Rathburn, Jim Price, and his eventual successor and protégé Dan Dickerson on radio. He also worked with Kaline and Jim Price on TV. And when Dickerson captured our imagination with his stirring call of Magglio Ordonez's pennant-clinching homer last October, Harwell couldn't have been any prouder.

Rizzs and Rathburn worked two tough years without Harwell's help when the Tigers and/or WJR foolishly tried to replace him in the early 1990s. Team president Bo Schembechler was vilified for the move, some say unjustly. But it was as silly a notion as trying to change the recipe for Coca-Cola.

Frank Beckmann did four seasons of radio with Lary Sorensen and Price. And though we associate Kell and Kaline with Tigers

TV, the crews have included Larry Osterman, Don Kremer, Joe Pellegrino, Mike Barry, Hank Aguirre, Norm Cash, Bill Freehan, Jim Northrup, Lance Parrish, Jack Morris, Dan Petry, Josh Lewin, and Kirk Gibson.

But when Dickerson and Price settled in on radio and Mario Impemba was joined by Rod Allen on television, Detroit was finally able to get past the "Where's Ernie?" and "I still miss Kell" complaints.

Allen became a cult figure in 2006 with his distinctive lingo for a "filthy" team and his "WOOOOO-EEEEE!" walkoff commentary. A drinking game even carried his name.

Dickerson and Impemba touched their listeners and viewers last season, proving once again an announcer can only be great in the public's mind when the team is—unless your name is Harwell and you'll never, ever be "looooong gone!"

Baseball in Detroit hasn't always been a day at the beach. Just check the standings. But Tigers baseball has been heard at the beach, in kitchens, on porches, in dens, in bedrooms, in all types of vehicles, during weddings, and in hospitals as patients' last breaths were drawn.

The sights and sounds can last a lifetime. The day you're born is Opening Day.

CHAPTER SEVENTEEN

The Walkoff Wonders

A WILD SUMMER OF LAST-CHANCE HEROICS

NO ONE ON EARTH COULD HAVE SEEN IT COMING. Former manager Sparky Anderson and FSN Detroit's Rod Allen say they did. But both were spotted with extraterrestrials just before the season began.

That's the only explanation for their clairvoyance concerning the 2006 Detroit Tigers. From 43 wins in 2003 to 72 the following season and from 71 victories in 2005 to 95 last year, the Motor City Kitties grew claws and scratched their way to the top.

For a franchise that hadn't won 80 games since Anderson's team won 85 in 1993 and hadn't been in postseason play since 1987, when rocket-armed reliever Joel Zumaya was just two years old, it all seemed surreal.

"If I told you I thought we'd be 30 games over .500 or whatever, that would be a total lie," American League Manager of the Year Jim Leyland said. "I thought we had some talent here. And we took some chances that worked out pretty well."

Pretty well? That's like saying a 76-36 mark on August 7 was pretty good. It was pretty for the 2006 Tigers and would've been gorgeous for the 1927 Yankees, though the last week of the regular season and part three of the postseason were letdowns.

"We took a pop on a couple of veterans who've done a nice job," Leyland said during the regular season. "We took a chance on a couple of kids with beaucoup talent. We had a couple of guys come out of nowhere. And knock on wood, we've been able to stay pretty healthy. That's why we're a big surprise. But we're also a pretty good team."

They were with the right guy leading the way. And that guy was Leyland, from the first day of spring training to the last game of the World Series. He set a different tone by reading his team the riot act for disrespecting a coach in March and reading its fragile psyche perfectly in early October.

After a 5-0 start in Kansas City and Texas, when every starter was 1-0, Detroit lost its home opener and was swept by the world champion White Sox. Worse yet, the Tigers were clubbed 10-2 by Cleveland on getaway day, a term they took far too literally.

The idea was to leave for a nine-game West Coast swing after they faced the Indians on Monday afternoon, April 17, a red-letter day—or at least a red-faced one.

"I was only there to do a Chris Shelton feature," Michigan Associated Press sports editor Larry Lage said of a first baseman who set an American League record with seven homers in his first 10 games. "But I got to the clubhouse quicker than normal. And for the only time all year, the door at the hallway was open. I could hear every word Leyland said. Let's just call it an obscenity-laced tirade. But it was the perfect example of what he didn't do in Colorado—put out the little fires."

Red Adair and Smokey the Bear couldn't have done better. And by the time he met the media for a few seconds in his office, Leyland had cooled to just below boiling.

"We stunk!" he barked. "Next question! … It was lackluster. The whole ball of wax was lackluster! We had a chance to take the series, take three out of four, and we came out like we brought our luggage to the park and had to play a game before we went on the road. That's not good enough!"

Pausing a split-second for oxygen, Leyland continued, "We stunk, period! … This stuff has been happening before. And it's not going to happen here! I'm not talking about anyone in particular. I'm talking about the team—myself, the coaches, and everybody else. It's my responsibility to have the team ready to play. And they weren't ready to play today. They were ready to get on the plane and go to Oakland. If they won, it was OK. And if they lost, it was okay. That's not good enough!'"

That postgame post-up did more for Detroit's psyche than anyone could have imagined, though FSN Detroit's Mario Impemba and franchise-saves king Todd Jones had an idea something special had just happened.

"It said, 'If you want to do it my way, let's go out and win a championship! If not, don't let the door hit you on the way out!'" Impemba said. "The players may have been a little surprised by that. But he let them know they weren't just here to pick up a paycheck and go through the motions. I think that was the turning point of the year."

"I think it did a lot to set the tone early," Jones said. "We knew he wasn't going to put up with anything. If we weren't going to play the right way, either we were going to be gone or he was going to be gone. And there was a good chance he wasn't leaving. He had a chance to establish that early. The rest is history. He backed up exactly what he said in early April and carried it through the season."

After a loss to the American League West Champion A's the following night made them 7-7, the Tigers won five in a row and were off and slugging. They were 28-7 over the next 43 days and began a habit of last-at-bat homers. That made them 35-14 on May 27. Three years earlier Detroit was 13-37 on that date and didn't win its 35th game until September 2.

"That's the best thing about our mindset," said third baseman Brandon Inge, a Tiger since 2001—longer than any current player or coach. "We don't care how many runs we're down now. We feel we're going to win, no matter what. Last night, we were down four early and still felt that way. When you win, it breeds that mentality."

So did some early attitude adjustments, especially a no-holds-barred harangue before Leyland's sanitized version for the media in mid-April.

"What he did that day is still here," rookie center fielder Curtis Granderson said. "He's not going to say something and forget about it. He keeps reminding you and pushing you. That's what the focus is and what it's going to be from day one to the end of the season. He's not going to accept anything less, even from the best-paid player on the team. If you're mentally ready to play every day, he'll be happy. If not …"

It was about a third of the way into the season that Inge suggested Leyland could return home to Pittsburgh. He wasn't trying to get rid of the president of the Brandon Inge Fan Club. He just wanted everyone to know "The Right Way to Play" had been established.

"When I heard that, I had my bags packed," Leyland said. "But I think he exaggerates. I don't have shit to do with it. They're good players. And they found out what it is to come in and have a purpose, a mission, and a plan. It was a helluva compliment for him to say I got them where they know what they're supposed to do. Remember, though, this isn't my first rodeo. I've been down this road before."

It may be the road less traveled in this day and age with astronomical contracts and agent demands. But it's still a well-worn path to success, as Jones, a veteran of 14 seasons in eight cities, was quick to say.

"The most important thing was he gave us an identity," Jones said. "He told us we were pretty good. When we started to play well, we bought into that. Pretty soon it's June, and we have a pretty good thing going. Then, it's August, and we're 40 games over .500. And that was all built in the very early days of spring training."

So was a philosophy that pitching and defense can do wonders—or become a team's undoing. No team in either league matched Detroit's 3.84 ERA or its 16 shutouts, despite just three complete games. And no American League team came within 90 chances of the Tigers' load defensively.

Free-agent signee and All-Star starter Kenny Rogers was 17-8 with a 3.84 ERA—though the real fun for him came in three postseason starts. And Rookie of the Year Justin Verlander was 17-9 with a 3.63 ERA, seventh best in the league.

Jeremy Bonderman was 14-9 with a 4.08 ERA and 202 strikeouts, second only to American League Cy Young Award winner Johan Santana. And hard-luck southpaw Nate Robertson was 13-13 with the same ERA as Rogers.

With lefty Mike Maroth limited to nine starts by an elbow that needed surgery and kept him out three months, Leyland and pitching coach Chuck Hernandez got by with fifth starters Zach Minor, 7-6 and 4.84, and Wilfredo Ledezma, 3-3 and 3.58.

Jones kept things exciting in his second stint as Detroit's closer and had a 3.94 ERA. He still tied for fourth in the league with 37 saves. But the big noise from the bullpen was Zumaya's

Tiger of the Year Carlos Guillen turns a double play as Alex Rodriguez of the New York Yankees slides. *(Photo by Rob Tringali/Sportschrome/Getty Images)*

fastball. Clocked as high as 103 mph, it popped mitts like M-80s. "Zoom-Zoom" was 6-3 with a 1.94 ERA in his first season.

Fernando Rodney led the Tigers with 63 appearances. He went 7-3 with seven saves and a 3.52 ERA. Lefty set-up man Jamie Walker had a 2.81 ERA in 56 games. And Jason Grilli ate innings and pitched in 51 games.

Rogers won his fifth Gold Glove and Ivan Rodriguez his 12th, breaking his record for catchers. Runners rarely tried to steal against "Pudge"—a show of respect that lowered the team ERA.

Inge led all American League third basemen with 398 assists, including enough spectacular play for a mini-clinic. Second baseman Placido Polanco had his team's best moment on defense with a shoulder separating, game-saving dive on a long pop-up in Boston. And left fielder Craig Monroe tied for second in American League outfield assists with 12.

Detroit's offense was as balanced as an accountant's checkbook. The Tigers hit 202 home runs, led by Monroe with 28, Inge with 27, left fielder-DH Marcus Thames with 26 in just 348 at-bats, and right fielder Magglio Ordonez with 24. Granderson and shortstop Carlos Guillen each added 19 dingers.

Guillen, voted Tiger of the Year, was ninth in the league with a .320 batting average and eighth with a .400 on-base percentage. And as he sat in front of his locker, the first one the media reached as it entered the clubhouse, Guillen was always ready to simplify the game in his broken English and unpretentious way.

Asked about his bizarre wardrobe, he smiled proudly and said of his shoes, "Walgreen's—$19.99!" And questioned about the bats he treated so lovingly before games, Guillen said, "To be a good bat, you've gotta hit some!"

It was hard to argue with Guillen's logic or Granderson's baseball growth chart. The Chicago native tied for third in the American League with nine triples and showed flashes of greatness. But Granderson wasn't the prototype leadoff hitter and had 174 strikeouts, third on Detroit's season list behind Cecil Fielder's 182 and Rob Deer's 175.

The Tigers left fewer runners on base than any American League team except Tampa Bay. And in the case of the Devil Rays, it was tough to strand runners with the bases empty.

It was tough for Detroit to know if its late heroics were sheer skill or somehow tied to "Gum Time," Robertson's chomping of Big League Chew wads in late innings. That contagious habit seemed to bring good luck.

But it didn't take superstitions for the Tigers to play four months of superior baseball, as seen by a 70-33 mark on July 29.

Some will always say the highlight was a 7-6, 10-inning triumph over Cincinnati on Saturday, May 20, the night Comerica Park changed forever. Others will point to 10 last-at-bat wins in the first three months. Even over the last two months, when a 10-game lead disappeared, Detroit had heroic homers from Rodriguez, Monroe, and Guillen.

That doesn't include the grand slam from Monroe that helped drop the White Sox to a third-place team or the subtle plays that winners make, like the slide into second base by Thames that might have meant more than any of his homers.

Eventually, as almost all teams do, the Tigers began to struggle. Some preferred another word and suggested a mass choke job as Minnesota crept ever closer.

"I don't pay any attention to that stuff and what the media says," Leyland said. "One guy says, 'The Tigers will fold.' Then, he says, 'Maybe they won't fold.' Then it's, 'It looks to me like the Tigers will hang in there.' The same guy said all three things. They're like anyone. They ride the wave. We might fold. We might not. Who knows?"

We all do now, blessed by 20-20 hindsight. Despite help from second-half acquisition Sean Casey at first base and September pickup Matt Stairs as a much-needed left-handed bat, Detroit faltered in the final weeks. And after clinching a berth in the playoffs with a win at Kansas City, the Tigers fell flatter than their dining-room tables by closing with five straight L's at home to Toronto and the Royals.

"We got ourselves into a bind with our pitching," Leyland said. "Four of our last five starts were terrible."

An excruciating 9-7 loss in 11 innings on the final Friday of the regular season was bad enough. But after a 9-6 defeat on the last Saturday, Detroit needed only to win on Sunday to be assured a piece of the Central Division title. Instead, a 10-8 giveaway in 12 innings left them in second place for the first time since May 16, a game behind the you-take-it-no-you-take-it Twins.

"We tried to give it to each other, and they finally took it," Leyland said. "I want to take the time to congratulate the Minnesota Twins. They won today when they had to, and we didn't. So I tip my hat to them. But I don't want to take anything away from what we've done. We didn't close the deal when we had chances, and it cost us the division title. But hey, we're still playing for a lot."

That instant realization when a somber clubhouse could have become a morgue might explain the reappearance of the 2006 Tigers over the next two weeks.

"Kind of a downer?" Rogers said, repeating a dumb question. "No, it's a BIG downer. Nobody should be happy or giggling about what went on here. Yeah, we're in the playoffs. But that's the fallback position. We have to understand what happened here so we can go out in the next series and play better."

For the Tigers to surrender 28 runs to Kansas City in three games almost suggests the invasion of the body snatchers—and the mind thieves, too. But Detroit's hearts were still beating. The beating of American League playoff teams was about to begin.

CHAPTER EIGHTEEN

The Yankee Killers

STUNNING THE EXPERTS, BUT NOT THEMSELVES

IT HAD ALL THE MAKINGS OF A MISMATCH. And that's … exactly what it was when the New York Yankees met the Detroit Tigers in the 2006 American League playoffs.

Wearing pinstripes: The top-seeded East Division champ, the winningest team in the American League regular season at 97-65 (20-13 since the start of its last series with Detroit on August 30), a feared franchise with 26 World Series winners, including four in the previous 10 years, and the best team a cash sequoia could buy, with a 40-player payroll of $207.5 million—not counting a $26 million luxury tax.

Wearing Tiger stripes: The slumping Central Division runner-up, a wild-card qualifier at 95-67 (13-18 in the previous five weeks), an organization that hadn't won more than 79 games since 1993 or a World Series in rookie sensation Joel Zumaya's lifetime and a fiscally sound franchise with a payroll of $89.8 million.

About the best thing anyone could say about Detroit's prospects was the defeatist line, "If we have to get past the Yankees anyway, it might be easier to do that now in a best-of-five series than later in a best-of-seven."

No one could have known what baffled New York third baseman Alex Rodriguez realized after Game 4—that if the teams had played seven times, the Tigers might have won six of them.

"We're in shock from the domination," a classy "A-Rod" said, answering every question an hour after his team was outscored 17-0 and held to a .119 batting average in a 20-inning span. "It seemed if we played three more games, they would've stuck it to us three more times. That's the frustrating part. They kicked our ass."

The national media had just decreed the Yanks would sweep through Detroit like another round of job cuts, make quick work of "Oak-esota" or whichever team survived an A's-Twins prelim, then meet the Mets in another Subway Series in Gotham.

They forgot to tell the Tigers, who devoured the Yanks like Subway sandwiches and set off a celebration worthy of a world championship, not a first-round romp.

To understand the shock of it all, remember Detroit had just dropped five in a row—two to Toronto and three to Kansas City—when one win at Comerica Park would have meant a division title. Instead of appearing at a Monday morning pep rally in their honor, Leyland's men were preparing to work out in New York.

"The first thing we've gotta do is regroup," Tigers pitcher Jeremy Bonderman said after a forgettable fizzle in Game 162. "Then, we've gotta find a way to win the series. We know it's a tough place to play. Somehow, we've gotta win one of the first two games there."

Or as Detroit first baseman and media magnet Sean Casey said, "It definitely hurt. That's the nature of the beast. But when we get showered and get on that flight, it's a new season. If we're going to have to beat the Yankees to get to our ultimate goal anyway, why not take them on in the first round?"

Who cared if the Tigers had won just two of seven games with New York in the regular season and were being given about as much chance as the Washington Generals have against the

Harlem Globetrotters? Not rookie center fielder Curtis Granderson.

"Not at all," Granderson said. "Everything is even again. We've seen wild-card teams move on and first-place teams move out. No matter what happened against K.C., we have to be ready to go Tuesday. All that changes is the opponent and the location. Everything else is the same."

Some would say that's like arguing the only difference between a puppy and a python is the number of legs. And it's safe to say the Yankees squeezed the dickens out of Detroit in Game 1, winning 8-4 on Tuesday night, October 3, in the Bronx.

Shortstop Derek Jeter, a Kalamazoo native, went 5-for-5 with two doubles and a solo homer, his 17th postseason shot. Right fielder and mid-summer care package Bobby Abreu drove in four runs. And designated hitter Jason Giambi homered, was hit by the pitch twice, and even stole a base.

Starting pitcher Chien-Ming Wang was staked to a 5-0 lead by the third inning. Detroit's Nate Robertson, who had held lefties to a league-low .181 average, was rocked from both sides of the plate by an All-Star lineup. Second baseman Robinson Cano became the first player to bat ninth in the postseason after finishing in the top three in hitting (.342.).

"That's why they've got the payroll they do," Robertson said. "They bring players in to do what they did tonight. They fight off the tough pitches and do damage other guys can't."

When Detroit manager Jim Leyland shook his head and said, "We just don't have that kind of firepower," he forgot to mention that neither does Smith & Wesson.

But leave it to Jeter to sound a captain's warning his teammates ignored with the comment, "Hey, it's a short series. We can't relax."

If Game 2 had been played on Wednesday evening as scheduled, New York's momentum might have given it a 2-0 lead and produced a different winner—or at least a Game 5 in Yankee Stadium.

After an exceptional 2006 season, Justin Verlander was named the American League Rookie of the Year. *(Photo by Andy Altenburger/Icon SMI)*

Instead, a weather postponement until Thursday afternoon gave the Tigers a chance to lick their wounds and scratch an overconfident foe. It didn't seem to matter that Detroit starter Justin Verlander started to warm up Wednesday, while New York's Mike Mussina had different information.

When it was time to shine, the American League Rookie of the Year pitched with the guile of a 10-time All-Star, fighting his way out of trouble for 5 ⅓ innings and allowing only a three-run homer to center fielder Johnny Damon in the bottom of the fourth.

Trailing 3-1 with five innings left in Game 2, Detroit had the Yankees right where it wanted them. As the hosts exhaled, the Tigers engineered their 34th and most important comeback of 2006. They tied it at 3 on Granderson's sacrifice fly in the fifth and shortstop Carlos Guillen's solo homer in the sixth. But the big blow was yet to come.

Detroit DH and Yankees reject Marcus Thames singled to lead off the seventh, went to second on a passed ball by catcher Jorge Posada, and moved to third on a sacrifice by third baseman Brandon Inge. With one out and the infield in, Granderson fell behind 0-2, fouled off two more pitches, then ripped a triple to the wall in left-center.

Leyland got 4 ⅔ innings of great relief work from Jamie Walker, Zumaya, and Todd Jones to seal the victory. Walker came on in the middle of an at-bat and got Cano to bounce into a double play. And with shadows encroaching, New York's hitters were helpless to handle Zumaya's heat, measured that day at 102 mph.

"Your instincts take over," Leyland said of his decision to bring Walker in with a 1-1 count. "And to be honest, I think we caught a big break. I don't want to take anything away from our club. But the shadows were pretty tough late in the game with a guy throwing 100 mph."

Leyland had said the matchup with the Yankees looked like the varsity against a freshman team. After squaring the series 1-1,

Zumaya suggested the Tigers had moved up to junior-varsity status.

When destiny's darlings returned to Comerica Park on a frosty Friday, the crowd was as electric as Detroit Edison. With "Mr. Tiger" Al Kaline throwing out the first ball and Kenny Rogers firing the rest, it was truly an evening to remember.

Back home, Leyland's concern before the series—handling the media and having the courage to say no—was finally a factor. Could that be tougher than facing Damon, Jeter, Abreu, Rodriguez, Giambi, Posada, Hideki Matsui, Bernie Williams, and Cano, with Gary Sheffield waiting to pinch hit? Maybe so, as easy as Rogers made it look.

"It's hard to say no when all of a sudden you've got 10,000 more friends than you thought you had, all wanting tickets," Leyland said. "You're getting people situated and making runs to the airport. If you get caught up in all those distractions, you're going to get your ass beat.

"I'm sure some people think I'm grumpy. I really don't give a shit. I don't want people making demands on the players to go to Joe's Hot Dog Stand to sign autographs when we're getting ready for the playoffs. I don't want to lead the league in appearances at Joe's Hot Dogs so people will say, 'Boy, those Tigers are really good in the community!' I want to win games! That's how you get people out here."

He couldn't have kept fans away from Game 3 if he had put a 10-foot-tall, barbed-wire fence around the ballpark. If a delirious crowd had been any louder, we may not have heard Rogers' self-psyching shrieks in a 6-0 masterpiece.

Scattering five hits in 7 ⅔ innings, he fanned eight with a full buffet of pitches, including a 94-mph fastball. Rogers, 41, beat cinch Hall of Famer Randy Johnson, 43, in an AARP-sponsored matchup and avoided decapitation with a Gold Glove snare.

"It was my pleasure to catch him today," Ivan Rodriguez said. "He didn't miss anything—changeups, fastballs, breaking balls, whatever I wanted. It was unbelievable."

"He was so emotional," Zumaya said. "He pitched his heart out. You can't ask for any more than he did tonight. And if that ball up the middle had been hit at me, I probably would've been dead."

Rogers had never been more alive on the mound. And his experience had never been more valuable, especially when he was a split second from a Rawlings tattoo.

"I'm pretty good at chuckin' and duckin'," he said. "But I was lucky to get my glove on that one. It hit me right in the pocket. It was a make-or-break play."

Four singles produced three Detroit runs in the second inning. "I-Rod" and Casey doubled in a two-run fifth. And Granderson ended the scoring in the sixth with his second homer of the week. That was more than enough support against a team that couldn't hang in Mr. Rogers' neighborhood.

"I don't think Kenny could've thrown the ball any better," Tigers president Dave Dombrowski said. "He has been such a quality individual since he has been with us. He has some ghosts in his background. But pitching like this against the New York Yankees in the postseason, I'm just absolutely thrilled for him and our club."

When told that 90 percent of the country was pulling for his team, Dombrowski smiled and said, "Well, let's hope we make them happy then!"

In the visitors' clubhouse Damon tried to put a brave face on a desperate situation, trailing 2-1 and facing elimination. His body language wasn't that convincing.

"We have our work cut out, but we have to believe we're the team to beat," Damon said. "It's all very shocking, not scoring for 14 innings. We're just kinda guessing what went wrong. But we're a good team. We'll come back tomorrow and win. We just need to try to get back to Yankee Stadium for Game 5."

As he trudged toward the exit, veteran pitcher Mike Mussina put it a different way, as a three-year graduate of Stanford would: "Our whole season is tomorrow. If we don't win, nothing else matters. The whole thing will be gone."

It vanished quicker than a Bonderman fastball. Retiring the first 15 hitters, he held New York to five hits in 8 ⅓ innings of an 8-3 win. Magglio Ordonez and Craig Monroe homered off Jared Wright, who was relieved in the bottom of the third by Cory Lidle—his last appearance before perishing in a plane crash.

"There's a special thing going on here," Bonderman said. "And we're going to try to ride it. Nobody gave us a shot! But these are the playoffs. Anything goes!"

"I want to give these fans a lot of credit," Monroe said. "They've been through the worst of times. And they've stuck by us. That's what makes this so sweet. Look at 'em! We beat the best team in baseball. And this is for them! Thank you, Detroit!"

They celebrated with cases and cases of G.H. Mumm champagne, spraying everything that moved. Some climbed into the stands. And if they hadn't had a date with Oakland, Guillen might still be on top of the Detroit dugout.

"It's a dream come true!" Casey said. "It's awesome! Jim Leyland told us we had to respect the Yankees but couldn't fear them. He said if we came out and played our game, we could win this series. And that's what we did!"

If anyone had more fun than Rogers, it had to be Thames, who spoke between dousings: "My wife told me this morning that today would be something special. And every time I play those guys, I want to beat them. I'm just being honest! They traded me away. And to be with the Tigers and knock them out, it feels great!"

Not if you were in or just outside the New York clubhouse, where senior vice president and G.M. Brian Cashman couldn't say enough about Detroit's performance.

"There are no guarantees in sports," he said. "But the Tigers were awesome—flat-out awesome! They have great ability. They were hungry. They wanted this series. And they took it. It's the age-old lesson. They led the league in ERA for a reason. Good pitching always beats good hitting. If we needed another history lesson, this was it."

A series for the ages. And 75 minutes after the game, three of the hundreds of signs in the stands said it all:

"Jeter can't handle our heater—No. 54!" (Zumaya)

"Leyland for President"

And most appropriately, "You Can't Buy Heart!"

CHAPTER NINETEEN

The Plays, Not The A's

A CLEAN SWEEP TO THE AMERICAN LEAGUE PENNANT

BASEBALL'S PLAYOFFS ARE NO PLACE FOR STYLE POINTS. The score can be 11-0 or 3-2. Postseason wins are counted, not graded. Yet, the 2006 Detroit Tigers got straight A's for a four-game sweep of Oakland in the American League Championship Series.

After stunning the once-mighty Yankees three games to one, the question for Jim Leyland's team was simple: "Are you satisfied yet?" The answer was almost as loud as the final crack of Magglio Ordonez's bat on October 14—exactly 22 years after a Game 5 win over San Diego in the 1984 World Series.

Ordonez's second homer of the day, a three-run shot off A's closer Huston Street in the bottom of the ninth at Comerica Park, gave the Tigers a final 6-3 triumph over the American League West Division Champions.

It also triggered a wild celebration for a wild-card team that had dared to dream. Since Kirk Gibson's clinching blast in 1984, only six franchises had failed to reach the World Series—Detroit, Baltimore, Milwaukee, Pittsburgh, Seattle, and Texas.

Even after winning 95 games, the fourth highest total in the majors, the Tigers were fourth on most lists as a prospective pennant winner. They were supposed to be slapped by New York in an American League Division Series. They had been passed on the final day of the regular season by Minnesota for the Central Division crown. And there was no reason to think they would obliterate Oakland, a 93 game-winner.

That mission began on Tuesday, October 10—a late-afternoon start in the Bay Area, but an evening game back in Michigan. It didn't matter. The sun had already set on the A's and Ken Macha, who would soon become the team's former manager.

Why that result was so hard for some to accept is still a mystery. Detroit had the No. 1 pitching staff in either league for six months. Its team ERA of 3.84 was significantly lower than Oakland's 4.21 mark. And the Tigers batted .274 with 203 homers, while the A's hit .260 with 175 dingers.

Apparently, the Tigers were punished in the court of public opinion for going 19-31 from August 8 through October 1. It was like an automotive recall on four months of fabulous play. And few recalled what had happened one year earlier. The 2005 Chicago White Sox had fought though a similar late-season slump and smiled all winter.

Detroit was ready to do just that with eight more triumphs. But everyone's attention was focused on the next four. The Mets and Cardinals would settle their squabble for National League supremacy without the Tigers' input.

"We'll have enough information," Leyland said. "I think too much is worse than too little. But it's still a matter of execution and doing things right. You can have all the information in the world. If a guy can't hit a low fastball but kills high fastballs and you make a mistake and throw one high, it's out of the park. So a scout can tell you till you're blue in the face. If you can't make the pitch, make the play, or hit a certain pitcher, it doesn't make any difference."

Leyland should know. After six seasons as a scout with St. Louis, he realized the value of his best reports depended on the people who read them. And he knew his players were baseball literate.

They understood one fundamental truth. Nothing that happened in nine regular-season games with Oakland would matter one bit in October. It was irrelevant that Detroit won five times, taking two of three at home and splitting six games on the road. The postseason was a different animal.

"They're just like we are," Leyland said. "They're gonna keep playing until the game's over. And they're one of the best teams in baseball. They just swept a great Minnesota team after the Twins came back and won our division. What does that tell you?"

It said if the Twins, with MVP Justin Morneau and batting champ Joe Mauer, could only score seven runs in three games, the Tigers might have to do more with less.

It also said one of the keys to success would be the same as it was for Detroit against the Yankees—respecting the A's but never fearing them.

"As long as we believe in ourselves, we can win," left fielder-DH Marcus Thames said. "But we have to go to Oakland first. They're an unsung team, the same way we are. They're going to be scrappy. And we're going to scrap right with them. We just have to play good baseball."

"That's exactly right," said rookie reliever Joel Zumaya, who would miss the next three games with a forearm injury from playing the video game *Guitar Hero*. "We don't have any pressure on us. We're just going to prove to people that we're competitive. And we're going to go right after them."

One of the other concerns, as it was against New York, became the demand for tickets from friends and forgotten acquaintances. Leyland spoke to that problem from personal experience before the playoffs began.

"I remember I paid a fortune for tickets somebody wanted," Leyland said. "When we lost a game, the guy said, 'I don't want the tickets for tomorrow. But I'll take them for the next day if you win!' So I got stuck with a couple thousand dollars in tickets. You know, it's not Santa Claus time!"

It was Christmas and New Year's and the Fourth of July rolled into one for the Tigers and some long-suffering fans. The fun began on the eve of the Series, when Leyland read his players an essay by his 14-year-old son, Patrick, on what defines a winner. The best part came when several players requested a copy.

If Leyland ever wanted to make copies of a win, the 5-1 domination in Game 1 in McAfee Coliseum would be an excellent candidate. The pitching of Nate Robertson, power and patience at the plate, and sharp defense set the tone for the next three games. And it more than paid the A's back for edging Detroit in five games in 1972.

The Tigers knocked Oakland ace Barry Zito out of the game after 3 ⅔ innings—his shortest of seven postseason starts and 15 career appearances against the Tigers. Zito retired the first eight Detroit hitters but just three of the next 13 before showering.

Third baseman Brandon Inge, 3-for-24 lifetime in that matchup, began the assault by pulling a high-and-tight fastball inside the foul pole in left for the week's first run.

Zito had 2-0 counts on the next three batters. Center fielder Curtis Granderson followed Inge's blow with a double. And second baseman Placido Polanco and first baseman Sean Casey drew full-count walks to load the bases.

When Ordonez's grounder to third was knocked down by Gold Glove winner Eric Chavez, the infield hit gave Robertson all the support he would need. And it wasn't the last game-winning RBI "Mags" would deliver.

Catcher Ivan Rodriguez made it 3-0 with a leadoff homer in the top of the fourth. And after Craig Monroe walked, Inge delivered an RBI double off the wall in left-center, again on a 2-0 pitch. Polanco, the Series MVP with a .529 average, made it 5-0 with an RBI single and signaled the end for baked Zito in an A's uniform.

"To be honest, I think playing the Yankees helped with our offensive approach," Leyland said. "We mentioned how patient the Yankees were and how they made the pitcher work. I think by talking about that so much, some of our guys picked up on it."

They also picked Robertson up with support. He had received more than three runs to work with in just 11 of 32 regular-season starts. But there was no need for "Gum Time" or other gimmicks—not when he opened with five shutout innings.

Robertson took care of that with clutch pitches and got a record-tying four double-play grounders. He escaped major trouble in the fourth, striking out the side after giving up a leadoff walk to Frank Thomas and a double to Jay Payton.

The only downer for the Tigers was a pulled calf muscle for Casey on a swing in the sixth. But Guillen made a smooth move to first and was in on DPs at two positions.

Another switch the following morning was the key to Game 2. Managing by feel rather than stats and scouting reports, Leyland made little-used Alexis Gomez his DH against Oakland starter Esteban Loaiza. A long home run and four RBIs later, Gomez was the hero and Leyland a genius in an 8-5 win.

It didn't matter that Thames had hit 26 homers in the regular season, 25 more than Gomez had belted in his major-league career. And the move wasn't made to get another left-handed hitter in the lineup against a veteran righty.

Leyland remembered that Gomez often looked great before the game. With the first pitch coming at about 5:15 p.m. Pacific time, why not see if Gomez's body clock might make him the man of the hour?

Usually, the idea is to simulate game conditions in batting practice. Leyland was hoping to do just the opposite, re-creating BP results under a postseason microscope.

"I told him, 'You're a great five o'clock hitter,'" Leyland said of a player with just six RBIs in 103 regular-season at-bats last year. "And he does have big-time power. Unfortunately, most of it comes during batting practice."

Gomez had tied an International League record on August 7 by hitting four home runs for Toledo in a win over Columbus. But he only needed a two-run single off Chavez's glove in the fourth to put his team ahead. A two-run shot to right in the sixth gave Gomez a place in baseball lore.

"That's why I'm here in the big leagues," Gomez said. "I'm not surprised."

After a moment of silence for Yankees pitcher and former A Cory Lidle, who died that day in a plane crash, Oakland responded with two home runs by center fielder Milton Bradley, one from each side of the plate.

But 17-game winner Justin Verlander and solid work from the bullpen helped put Detroit in a commanding position. All eight playoff teams that had won the first two games on the road had advanced to the World Series.

The Tigers were about to make it 9 for 9. Back home, it was time for one of the best pitching performances in postseason history, followed by a power surge.

As good as Rogers was against New York, he was better in another Game 3 on a fabulous Friday. He surrendered just two hits in 7 ⅓ innings, including a single by catcher Jason Kendall to start the game. Rogers' scoreless string in the 2006 playoffs had reached 15 innings on its way to 23.

"He's a professional pitcher, that's what he is," Leyland said. "There are guys with better stuff and guys who'll light up the radar gun. But nobody could've pitched better than Kenny did in these last two outings."

The Tigers got all the runs they needed in the first when Rich Harden began by throwing seven straight balls. After Granderson's walk, Monroe's single put runners at first and third with none out. Polanco had the game-winning RBI with a single. And Ordonez made it 2-0 by hitting into a force out—no sense in wasting his thunder.

Monroe made it 3-0 and capped the scoring with a homer to lead off the fifth. By that point Rogers was rolling to his 11th win in 12 decisions against Oakland since 2002.

Saturday's game was a different type of triumph. Detroit trailed for five-and-a-half innings, more than it had in its previous six wins combined. And that only made it sweeter when Ordonez snapped out of a 2-for-15 slump and fulfilled two promises—one to an organization that believed in him and one to a son who adored him.

Craig Monroe (left), Curtis Granderson (middle), and Magglio Ordonez get together in the outfield during a pitching change. *(Photo by Jed Jacobsohn/Getty Images)*

Overcoming a 3-0 deficit and watching Jeremy Bonderman get better with each inning, the Tigers chipped away in the fifth on RBI doubles by Granderson and Monroe. That set the stage for Ordonez to open the sixth with a tying drive down the left-field line.

Three innings later, after Monroe and Polanco singled, Ordonez responded again on a 1-0 fastball, as Dan Dickerson described in an unforgettable call on the Detroit Tigers Radio Network:

"Swing and a fly ball, left field. It's deep! It's way back! … THE TIGERS ARE GOING TO THE WORLD SERIES! THREE-RUN WALKOFF HOME RUN! OHHH, MAN!

ORDONEZ AROUND THIRD! HE'S INTO A MOB SCENE AT HOME! THE TIGERS HAVE BEATEN THE A'S 6-3, COMPLETING A FOUR-GAME SWEEP IN ONE OF THE GREATEST TURNAROUNDS IN BASEBALL HISTORY!"

Though he hit .298 with 24 homers and a team-high 104 RBIs in 2006, Ordonez was capable of more. And on the 11th birthday of Magglio Jr., we learned what that was.

"I told him, 'I'm going to hit a home run for you,'" Ordonez said as the delirium continued. "Instead, I hit two. After the game I said, 'This is your gift!'"

His team had just set a major-league record by winning six straight postseason games by three runs or more. No other team had won more than four in a row by that margin.

Detroit set another mark when Leyland became the first manager to win three straight playoff games with different starters at shortstop—Guillen, Neifi Perez, and Ramon Santiago.

The second baseman never changed anything but his hooded sweatshirt. Twenty-seven days after he told the media he was done for the season, Polanco answered a silly "How does it feel?" question the only way he could: "Oooh! What do you think?"

Better than a separated shoulder. Just not as good as four more wins would.

CHAPTER TWENTY

The Tigers-Cards, Part III

2006 WORLD SERIES MEMORIES

IT TOOK SIX AND A HALF MONTHS and 170 games for the Detroit Tigers to win the American League pennant. And with 102 wins in that span, including seven in eight tries in the playoffs, they finally did the unfathomable. A franchise that hadn't won 80 games since 1993 won enough respect to be favored in the World Series.

Detroit's opponents, the St. Louis Cardinals, had only the fifth-best record in the National League at 83-78. The Central Division survivors needed seven games to get past the New York Mets in the National League Championship Series. And they ranked behind the Tigers in virtually every significant stat:

	DETROIT	ST. LOUIS
	HITTING	
Runs scored	822	781
Hits	1,548	1,484
Total bases	2,531	2,382
Doubles	294	292
Triples	40	27
Home runs	203	184
Average	.274	.269
Stolen bases	60	59

	DETROIT	ST. LOUIS
PITCHING		
Wins	95	83
Saves	46	38
Shutouts	16	9
ERA	3.84	4.54
Strikeouts	1,003	970
Hits allowed	1,420	1,475
Walks allowed	489	504
Homers allowed	160	193

All of which goes to show how little statistics can mean in a best-of-seven—or in the Tigers' case, a worst-of-five.

There's no shame in being the second-best team in baseball in October. It sure beats being the second-best team in the ballpark 119 times, as Detroit was three years earlier. And 28 of the other 29 teams would pay to trade places.

The problem comes when you know you could have done better. And no insult to the Redbirds, who won the four games they had to win by a combined score of 21-8. But every time the Tigers have heard the words "2006 World Champions" since October 27, they probably think, "That should have been us!"

Few will remember that St. Louis' 78 losses were the most for any World Series winner—or that the Cardinals were just the second team since the three-round playoffs began in 1995 to claim the crown without ever having home-field advantage.

They will recall how Detroit's bats went AWOL and its pitchers forgot how to field for a week. That's the only regret—that St. Louis never faced the Tigers, who had taken baseball by storm and become the feel-good story of the season.

Detroit manager Jim Leyland and Cardinals skipper Tony La Russa felt good about their teams and just as strongly about each other when the games began on Saturday night, October 21, in Comerica Park, shortly after Bob Seger's rendition of "America the Beautiful." Their friendship would be strengthened by the week's events.

The Tigers got to open at home because the American League had won the 77th All-Star Game, 3-2. And that seemed like an edge for a team that had gone 50-35 at home, including the playoffs, and 8-1 there against the National League Central. That included a three-game sweep of the Cardinals—10-6, 7-6 in 10 innings, and 4-1—from June 23-25.

Two rookies started on the mound in Game 1 for the first time in World Series history. And an Anthony Reyes-vs.-Justin Verlander matchup seemed to favor the hosts, especially when Craig Monroe doubled, Magglio Ordonez walked, and Carlos Guillen singled for a 1-0 lead in the bottom of the first.

But in the top of the second, third baseman Scott Rolen led off with a long homer to left to make it 1-1. Rolen was 0-for-15 in past World Series, setting a record for futility. That was quickly forgotten with one swing of the bat.

St. Louis broke through in the third with three runs and silenced an overflow crowd of 42,479. Chris Duncan's RBI double scored lead-footed Yadier Molina for a 2-1 lead. On the next delivery, 2005 National League MVP Albert Pujols hit a two-run, opposite-field shot for a three-run lead.

Late in the regular season, Leyland had talked in glowing terms about the Cardinals' top threat, a player he had watched develop during six years as a Pittsburgh-based scout for St. Louis.

"In all my years of baseball I've never seen anyone like him," Leyland said. "(Barry) Bonds is the best player I've ever had. For the last several years he has probably been the best player in the game. But this guy now … I was with the Cardinals when he came up in spring training. I'll never forget (pitching coach) Dave Duncan was the only guy who voted to keep him on the team. And the point he made was true. This guy never swung at a bad pitch the entire spring. I couldn't believe it."

A lot of people couldn't believe that Pujols had a chance to swing at anything. With first base open and two outs, why not walk him and pitch to Juan Encarnacion? That's what should have happened if Verlander's fastball hadn't tailed back toward the edge of the plate, a pitch Leyland said was his fault.

"The manager's decision is either to pitch to him or walk him," he said. "I pitched to him. Obviously, he burned us. I'm not going to get into a lot of explanation about what the thinking was. But I take the bullet there. If somebody gives criticism, I accept it."

It was one of the few times all season that Leyland had been wrong or the execution of a single pitch had been so costly. But that delivery wasn't the only problem.

Reyes, whose five regular-season wins were the lowest for a Game 1 starter in World Series history, suddenly looked like Bob Gibson and retired 17 straight hitters from the first inning to the sixth.

The Cardinals added three more runs in that inning to make it 7-1. The Tigers made three errors in the game, including two by third baseman Brandon Inge—a wild throw to the plate and obstruction of a runner heading home—on the same play.

Monroe connected for a solo homer in the bottom of the ninth, just the fourth Detroit hit off Reyes, who immediately gave way to Braden Looper. But a 7-2 win was the first in a World Series for the National League in three years and the first for St. Louis in 19.

For those who said it would be a cold day in Caracas before the Tigers dropped two in a row at home to the Cardinals, the 40-degree temperature at Comerica Park must not have reached Venezuela.

The fun started when superfan Anita Baker sang the national anthem and former manager Sparky Anderson flew in from California to throw out the first ball. It was the only hittable offering St. Louis would see for a while.

Kenny Rogers was brilliant on the mound again, allowing two hits in eight shutout innings of a Series-tying 3-1 win. And Todd Jones got the save after a scary ninth, retiring Jim Edmonds on a bases-loaded force at second.

But the attention was focused on an unknown smear or smudge near the base of Rogers' left thumb. That was quickly pointed out by Fox baseball analyst Tim McCarver, best known to Detroit fans as the hitter who popped up to fellow catcher Bill Freehan to trigger the '68 celebration.

After an out against the St. Louis Cardinals in Game 2 of the 2006 World Series, starting pitcher Kenny Rogers celebrates. *(Photo by Ron Vesely/MLB Photos via Getty Images)*

La Russa didn't view "Dirtgate" as a Cardinal sin. He just wanted the substance gone. That was where most of his hitters were, too, on Sunday night, October 22, when Rogers stretched his scoreless streak to 23 innings in the 2006 postseason.

"It was dirt and resin and all that stuff mixed together," Rogers said. "When it's moist, it stays on your hand. I wiped it off. I didn't know it was there. But they told me, and I took it off after the first inning. I didn't think it was an issue. But if it distracts someone …"

If Rogers was in the St. Louis players' heads, his teammates were all over the bases with 10 hits. Guillen was a homer away from a cycle. And Monroe supplied that, joining Jimmie Foxx in 1929, Dusty Rhodes in 1954, Ted Simmons in 1982, and Bonds in 2002 as the fifth player with dingers in his first two World Series games.

A crowd of 42,533 enjoyed every second. And as St. Louis outfielder Preston Wilson said, "I don't think I've seen this many people with cat faces painted on since … I don't know, *Cats* in New York. This is crazy!"

But with a split in the two games at Comerica, the Tigers lost the home-field advantage. Three games later, they lost the Series. And no one with tickets for Game 6 or 7 knew Detroit had just played its final home game of 2006.

As good as Rogers had been, Cardinals ace Chris Carpenter was just as strong in Game 3, a 5-0 win in the first World Series game played in the new Busch Stadium. The 2005 Cy Young Award winner allowed three hits, didn't walk a batter, and threw just 82 pitches in eight innings on Tuesday night, October 24.

St. Louis got all the runs it needed on Jim Edmonds' bases-loaded double in the fourth off Nate Robertson. The Cardinals made it 4-0 in the seventh on a two-run throwing error by relief pitcher Joel Zumaya. The final run scored on a wild pitch.

Game 4 was delayed a day by rain that fell mainly on the plains. But whatever the Tigers did on that unexpected day off, it didn't work nearly as well as the postponement in New York. It also didn't include an extra hour of PFP—pitchers' fielding practice.

In the key matchup of the Series, the one Detroit had to win and would play over and over in its nightmares with the same result, St. Louis prevailed 5-4. The Cardinals weren't great—just good enough to take what was given to them.

The Tigers led 3-0 entering the bottom of the third. Sean Casey had two RBIs, including a solo homer. And Ivan Rodriguez singled home Guillen in a 3-for-4 night after going hitless for three games.

St. Louis chipped away with runs in the third and fourth innings on RBI doubles by Series MVP David Eckstein and Molina—an omen of what was to come on wet turf.

Eckstein's second double, a seventh-inning shot over the head of a slipping Curtis Granderson in center, was reminiscent of Jim Northrup's triple past Curt Flood in '68. And Eckstein scored when reliever Fernando Rodney fired So Taguchi's sacrifice bunt over Polanco's head. When Wilson added a two-out single, the Cardinals led 4-3.

Detroit tied it at 4 in the eighth when Inge doubled home Rodriguez. But Eckstein, generously listed at 5-foot-7 and 165 pounds, scored Aaron Miles with the winning run in the bottom of the eighth. His double to left-center glanced off the glove of a diving Monroe and gave St. Louis reliever Adam Wainwright the win over Zumaya.

The rain stopped on Friday just long enough to play Game 5. And Verlander appeared to have dodged a storm when he walked three batters and launched two wild pitches. An outstanding play by Guillen at short stranded three runners.

The Cardinals scored in the second, however, when Inge made a great stop on Eckstein's blast down the line, then threw wildly to first, scoring Molina.

The Tigers took their last lead of the season in the fourth when right fielder Chris Duncan misplayed Ordonez's short fly to right-center. When Casey pulled the next pitch just inside the foul pole in right, Detroit was ahead 2-1.

After Molina and Taguchi singled in the bottom of the fourth, ex-Tiger pitcher Jeff Weaver tried to drop a sacrifice bunt. When Verlander failed to set his feet and fired the ball past Inge at third, the game was tied. And Eckstein promptly gave his team its Series-clinching run with an RBI groundout.

The Cardinals made it 4-2 and ended the scoring in the seventh when Rolen singled in the omnipresent Eckstein. That was more than Wainwright needed, though a double by Casey and a walk to Polanco brought the go-ahead run to the plate. Dreams of one more comeback died when Inge struck out on three pitches.

Detroit allowed eight unearned runs, with its pitchers committing a World Series-record five errors. There was a reason the fans at Busch held signs that read, "Hit it to the pitcher!" And the first three men in the batting order combined to bat .103, including an 0-for-17 from Polanco.

"We were forced to make plays we make in our sleep, and we didn't make them," Jones said. "But it's a great experience for a lot of us. If this doesn't show you that little things win championships, I don't know what will."

It was an excruciating reminder, one that will carry over to 2007 and beyond. If the Tigers didn't quite get to the summit, they still shocked the world. And they have a strong foothold for several more climbs. The champagne will keep.

CHAPTER TWENTY-ONE

The Future Is Now

THE 2006 ROOKIES AND
THE NEW-LOOKING TIGERS

"THOSE WHO DON'T LEARN FROM HISTORY are destined to repeat it," the saying goes.

The Detroit Tigers can only hope so in two important ways this season. They lost to the St. Louis Cardinals in the 1934 World Series, then bounced back to beat the Chicago Cubs the following year for the franchise's first championship.

The last time we checked, the Cardinals were still claiming victory over the Tigers in October 2006. It's up to Detroit to respond again. And almost any team would take another 103 wins, counting eight in postseason play. A repeat performance would be fine with the Tigers—with two quick do-overs.

If Detroit could have the final five games of the regular season and the last four days of the World Series back, it would welcome a rerun of everything else.

Why not? With the best pitching in baseball last year and the potential to be better in 2007, the Tigers have a leg up on every opponent. Ask the Yankees and A's. Or why not check with the champions?

"What they did was a great story," St. Louis manager Tony La Russa said. "And they're not just a good team now. They're going to be good for a while."

Perhaps Jim Leyland's club will plateau. Maybe injuries will hit even harder than they did with the loss of pitcher Mike Maroth for three and a half months and second baseman Placido Polanco for 37 days.

But for every player who had a career year—Marcus Thames, please take a bow—several of his teammates can play a lot better.

First baseman Sean Casey, who batted .305 in nine National League seasons, should hit a lot better than his .245 mark in 53 games with Detroit. The three-time All-Star with Cincinnati won't miss six weeks with two fractures in his lower back this time.

Center fielder Curtis Granderson should continue to grow in his second full season and won't strike out 174 times, 20 more than anyone in the American League. Unless the sophomore jinx hits one of the team's smartest players, expect significant improvement.

And pitcher Nate Robertson, whose ERA has plunged roughly 0.50 each year since 2003, is due to finish better than 13-13. He had the same ERA as All-Star starter Kenny Rogers and a better hits-per-innings ratio than Justin Verlander or Jeremy Bonderman.

"We should have another good team," Hall of Famer and special assistant to the president Al Kaline said. "Not only do we have some good young pitchers here, we have quality arms in the minor leagues. And whenever you have a lot of good pitchers, other teams want them. If you have a need, there's always the possibility you could trade somebody or a couple of people for the one or two guys you need to fill out your lineup."

For 22 seasons with the Tigers, Kaline always seemed to know where the ball was headed. And his comments the last day of the season showed his instincts were as sharp as ever. On November 11, Detroit sent oft-injured pitching prospect Humberto Sanchez and Class A relievers Kevin Whelan and Anthony Claggett to New York for feared slugger Gary Sheffield.

"We needed one more quality hitter in the middle of our lineup," Tigers president, CEO, and general manager Dave

Dombrowski said in early January. "We did a lot of checking on him and had to give up some talent to get him. But that was the strength of our organization. We're still deep there. And this gives us a real chance."

Sanchez, just a 31st-round draft pick in 2001, was 10-6 last year with a combined 3.29 ERA for AA Erie and AAA Toledo. Whelan was 4-1 with 27 saves and a 2.67 ERA for Lakeland. And Claggett was 7-2 with 14 saves and an 0.91 ERA for West Michigan.

If any of those players has half the career Sheffield has had, he'll never have to work another day after his final pitch. At age 38, the nine-time All-Star and former National League batting champion is still a force in any lineup, provided he's healthy.

Among active players, Sheffield ranks sixth in walks (1,293), seventh in being hit by the pitch (119), eighth in runs (1,433), hits (2,390), and RBIs (1,501), and ninth in home runs (455). He's 31st on the all-time homers list, three ahead of Hall of Famer Carl Yastrzemski. And his career batting average is .297 in 19 seasons with the Brewers, Padres, Marlins, Dodgers, Braves, and Yankees.

Sheffield should be an everyday DH for the Tigers, but could play some right field to relieve Magglio Ordonez. Two things are certain. He won't play first base, as he tried to do to help New York. And he won't publicly criticize Leyland as he did Yankees manager Joe Torre.

"Gary knows Jim very well from his days with Florida," Dombrowski said, recalling that Sheffield's fifth year with the Marlins and Leyland's first ended with a World Series celebration. "That relationship is very important here. Jim had a lot of input in the move and can handle different personalities."

If successful managing is 20 percent strategy and 80 percent psychology, Leyland holds a Ph.D. in both. After controlling a young Kirk Gibson in the Tigers farm system and pushing Barry Bonds to greatness in Pittsburgh, it was no surprise that he and Sheffield had a good relationship and better results in 1997.

"You've gotta treat everybody the same within the parameters of the team," Leyland said. "But you've gotta treat everybody different, too. I think each player should have his own identity. I'm all for that. And I wouldn't give you a nickel for a player who wasn't a little selfish. I want a guy who wants to be up there with the damn bases loaded! I don't want somebody who's hiding."

Sheffield has never hid from the spotlight. And he won't be able to do that in the heart of Detroit's order, probably in the No. 3 hole. But if a guy can't get along in the Tigers clubhouse, he can't be part of a lot of teams.

"For whatever reason, some personalities seem to hit it off a little better than others," Leyland said, referring primarily to free agents. "I think that holds true with teammates, coaches, trainers, and managers. I understand the dollars are the most significant thing. But some players feel comfortable with a certain organization and say, 'That's where I'd like to be.' For whatever reason, there seems to be a little better rapport than somewhere else."

That's what everyone is hoping with a player who was limited to 39 games last season by injuries. With a two-year contract extension through 2009, Sheffield will earn $41 million for the next three seasons. But with his wrist healed and his mind right, Detroit is more than ready to take that risk.

"I don't believe anybody knows how much any of us has left," Dombrowski said. "You make the best decision you can and do everything to have a good off-season. But you never really know 100 percent. Anybody can break down at any point."

Breaking down the 2007 Tigers, the 23-year-old Verlander should be ready to build on his Rookie of the Year season. If he doesn't become the first Detroit player to win 20 games since Bill Gullickson in 1991, it'll only be because a teammate beats him to it.

At 17-9, Verlander tied for fourth in the league in wins and had the most victories in a Tigers debut since Mark Fidrych's 19 in 1976. He was seventh in American League ERA at 3.63 and had the second-best fastball in the league, according to *Baseball America*.

Rogers' 17-8 mark and 3.84 ERA was just a tease for what was to come in three shutout starts in the postseason, giving him 20 wins the hard way. He won six straight starts from August 17 to September 23 and seemed to get stronger as the year progressed.

At age 42, Rogers has the savvy to pitch, not just throw, beyond 2007, the final year on his contract. Expect him to stretch his string of 23 straight shutout innings in the playoffs this October.

Bonderman drove Leyland nuts at times, including the final day of the regular season, because he's capable of consistent excellence. At 14-8 with a 4.08 ERA, he knows what the future can bring. And armed with a four-year, $38-million contract, the 24-year-old should mature into a solid No. 2 starter.

"They gave me a good offer that will keep my family comfortable," Bonderman told the Associated Press in December. "We had a lot of success this year. And I get along with the players and the coaching staff, so this wasn't really that hard of a call for me."

Joining the hard-luck Robertson, 29, should be a healthy Maroth, less than a month older. With a surgically repaired elbow, he could be the best fifth starter in baseball and part of a balanced staff with three lefties in the rotation.

That doesn't count southpaws Wilfredo Ledezma, 25, and 2006 first-round selection Andrew Miller, who debuted last summer at age 20. Ledezma had a 3.58 ERA, lower than Verlander's. And Miller, a star at North Carolina, nearly became the first draft pick to pitch in the College World Series and the Fall Classic in the same season.

Living in the Renaissance Center but eating most of his meals at Comerica Park after an August 30 debut in Yankee Stadium, the 6-foot-6 Miller is ranked as the No. 2 prospect in the organization. If Rogers ever decides to retire, Miller should be a great replacement. Think Mark Mulder with a better fastball and better health.

Detroit fans expect "Zoom-Zoom" Joel Zumaya to have a stellar sophomore season with the Tigers. *(Photo by Andy Altenburger/Icon SMI)*

Throw in last year's No. 5 starter, righty Zach Minor, a respectable 7-6 in his major-league debut, plus heralded AAA prospect Jordan Tata, both 25, and it's easy to see why Sanchez was expendable.

"We've got a pretty good baseball team and a chance to get better within the next five years," Leyland said. "We've got a chance to be good for a while. We've got pitchers stacked up pretty good. I'm talking about the minor leagues, too."

Jones isn't ready to step aside yet. And with 263 major-league saves, including 179 with Detroit, he can joke that his secret is getting batters out before they realize he doesn't have anything. But he has had enough to save 77 games the past two seasons.

His apparent heir as closer is Mr. Guitar Hero himself, Joel Zumaya. With a fastball that has topped out at 103 mph, his potential is matched only by his exuberance.

"Hey, Todd is Detroit's all-time greatest closer, dude!" Zumaya said. "I have no problem with that. And we're a good combination. Todd's stuff is a lot different from mine. I'll go right after you. I'm not afraid of anyone. That's just the way I pitch."

At age 22, Zumaya might be a better long-range prospect than Verlander or top-rated Cameron Maybin, a five-tool center fielder with West Michigan. Zumaya has more than enough confidence. And his changeup that turned Chicago's Jermaine Dye from a man to a mannequin for an August strikeout might have been Detroit's Pitch of the Year.

He finished 6-3 with a 1.94 ERA. But the first clue Zumaya was special came after one of his worst moments, a fastball that Ken Griffey Jr. blasted into orbit for a game-tying grand slam on Saturday, May 20, 2006.

"Granderson homered to win it in 10," Detroit talk-radio host Mark Wilson remembered. "Anyway, the last guy out of the training room is Zumaya. He starts screaming to Brian Britten, the media relations manager, 'Did you call the hospital?' Brian says, 'What are you talking about?' And Zumaya says, 'Did you call the hospital? I want to know how the guy is who got plunked

in the head with the speed of that pitch that hit Griffey's bat!'
Brian says, 'Now that's why this kid gets it.' He was happy they
won. He gave up a tape-measure shot and moved on. But he'll
remember that forever."

The Tigers also have Fernando Rodney and Jason Grilli as set-
up men and innings eaters. But they had to replace left-hander
Jamie Walker, who signed with the Orioles for $11 million.
Dombrowski thinks he might have done that on December 10 by
adding aging righty Jose Mesa at a fraction of the cost.

"We didn't want to lose Jamie," Dombrowski said. "But we
weren't prepared to pay those dollars. We can use Ledezma there.
And Mesa should help. Ideally, you'd want another left-hander
there. But the big thing is whether he can get guys out."

When Maybin, Miller, and the next wave arrive, players like
Granderson, Verlander, and Bonderman should be young
veterans. But the farm system has to keep churning. Detroit
would like to sign shortstop Carlos Guillen, the team's MVP, to
a multiyear deal, as it just did with third baseman Brandon Inge.
And there is no heir apparent for Guillen, 31, or All-Star catcher
Ivan Rodriguez, 35, waiting on-deck.

"You're always aware that you might have to replace players,'
Dombrowski said. "We know 'Pudge' isn't going to catch
forever."

As long as he does, Rodriguez bears watching—for a lot of
reasons.

"I tell the younger guys here, 'Just watch 'Pudge' and how he
goes about his business. He'll teach you how to get ready,'"
special assistant to the president Willie Horton said. "That's what
I learned from Kaline and those guys. But you have to keep the
little boy in you. When you don't have that, you should retire."

The guy who can't retire yet is Leyland. And after an
invigorating return to the dugout, there's no sign he wants to
walk away again.

"Trading is the general manager's job," Leyland said. "I don't
want to get into that. But I will say we're going to do whatever
we can to make this better for however long I'm here—and I

hope that's at least five years. The goal is to get the Tigers where you go to spring training every year and know you have a chance. And this is a good club. It has that chance."

It has more than a chance. It's a defending league champ. A hundred years after Detroit's first title, could there be a better way to honor that memory and the men who wore the olde English "D" than to sip some freshly opened champagne?

INDEX

Celebrate the Heroes of Michigan Sports
in These Other Releases from Sports Publishing!